KING ME

KING ME

STEVE FARRAR

MOODY PUBLISHERS

CHICAGO

Scripture quotations, unless otherwise indicated, are taken from the
New American Standard Bible®, Copyright © The Lockman Foundation 1960, 1962,
1963, 1968, 1971, 1972, 1973, 1975, 1977, 1995. Used by permission.

Scripture quotations marked NIV are taken from the *Holy Bible, New International
Version.*® NIV.® Copyright © 1973, 1978, 1984 by International Bible Society.
Used by permission of Zondervan Publishing House. All rights reserved.

ISBN: 0-8024-3321-9
EAN/ISBN-13: 978-0-8024-3321-3

3 5 7 9 10 8 6 4 2

Printed in the United States of America

TO JOHN AND JOSH

If I were to leave this earth today
I would go knowing that you are ready
And committed to follow the Lord and lead your future families.
I couldn't be more proud of you guys.
He has great things in store for both of you.

"For I am confident of this very thing,
That He who began a good work in you will perfect it..."
Philippians 1:6

CONTENTS

ACKNOWLEDGMENTS

I owe a great debt to Greg Thornton and Mark Tobey for their understanding and patience as this book developed and took some unexpected twists. Their flexibility and trust made a great difference as this book was taking a different shape than I originally envisioned. They are both men of faith and they demonstrated it through every phase of this work.

My wife, Mary, is my first editor in all of my writing projects. Her wisdom and insight are a tremendous benefit. And her desk is just on the other side of my office door. So we're able to discuss and talk over chapters without picking up the phone or sending e-mail. That's a great arrangement. And she is to be congratulated for coming up with the superb cover concept.

I want to thank both my sons, John and Josh, for allowing me to put into print some of the struggles we went through as a family. There is a very fine line in knowing what to say and what not to say. I am grateful to both of them for giving their permission to allow those outside of our family to hear about some of the difficulties we went through—and the goodness of God in making a way for all of us. We are stronger as a family as a result of those hard times and for that I'm grateful.

Augustine said it best: "God would never permit evil, if He could not bring good out of evil."

We've experienced that goodness firsthand. And so will you.

The most decisive actions of our lives—I mean

those that are most likely to decide the whole course of

our future—are, more often than not, unconsidered.

—ANDRE GIDE

CHAPTER ONE

KING ME

HIS LIFE COULD NOT HAVE BEEN GOING ANY BETTER.

And then the phone rang.

He was an evangelist who preached the Word with the Holy Spirit's authority and power. He was the most sought-after evangelist in his denomination. If you wanted him to come and preach in your church, you had to get in line and wait for a minimum of four years. He was a man who was enjoying the favor of God on his life and ministry.

The numerous invitations were always a pull away from his family. But he and his wife had settled on a formula that had worked well and enabled him to spend time at home with his bride and son that he dearly loved. The formula was simple: He would go out and preach for two weeks and then come home for two weeks. And then he would go out again for two weeks and back home for another two. Everything was working and God was blessing. His marriage was strong. His boy, now a teenager, was doing well in school and athletics. And his ministry was taking off like a rocket.

And then the phone rang.

It was a very short phone call from his wife. She had just had the latest in a series of arguments with their sixteen-year-old son. She had asked him to do something and he told her point-blank that he wasn't going to do it. This six-foot-two boy was wearing her down. His strong will was starting to take its toll. So she called her husband and in a fairly short conversation reported the events that had just taken place. And then she simply said, "I need you." He replied that he would cancel the remaining meetings and drive home immediately. Neither one of them knew that their son was listening to their conversation from the next room. The teenager knew he was pushing the limits and was curious to see how his father would respond. He would soon find out.

His father arrived home and within days a For Sale sign was in the front yard. The father then cancelled every one of his scheduled meetings for the next four years and accepted the pastorate of a small church in another state. For the next two years, until his son graduated from high school and went off to college, he pastored the small church and mentored his growing son.

With his son headed off to college, he was ready to return to evangelism. But in those few years multiple changes had taken place in his church denomination. Many of the older pastors had retired and been replaced by younger men who were unfamiliar with his ministry. Invitations were less frequent. Those few years away from evangelism had cost him dearly in terms of his career and calling. Quite frankly, to a degree, he would never recover. The decision to go home had come at a great price.

But because he had made the tough decision and went home to

focus on his family, years later his son would begin a ministry known as Focus on the Family.

I recently had the privilege of ministering with Dr. James Dobson during a weeklong conference sponsored by Focus on the Family. And when Dr. Dobson told the story about the decision his father had made, I knew it was the opening for this book.

James Dobson is the product of his father, James Dobson Sr. The elder Mr. Dobson was a man who knew his biblical priorities. That was the motivation that led him to make the decision to build his son before he built his ministry. Few men would have the courage or the conviction to make such a step. But aren't you glad that he did? I know that Dr. Dobson is.

James Dobson Sr. had a wonderful wife and James Dobson Jr. had a wonderful mother. She was a godly and capable woman. She loved both her husband and son and would do anything for them. And she did. But she was wise enough to know when she had reached her limitations. That's when she called her husband.

As great a woman as she was, she knew that she couldn't mentor their son. That was something only her husband could do. And he knew it too. So he bit the bullet, denied himself, said no to the crowds and to the invitations, and went home to do the work that only a man can do.

The Lord Jesus said in Matthew 16:24–25,

> **"If anyone wishes to come after Me, he must deny himself, and take up his cross and follow Me. For whoever wishes to save his life will lose it; but whoever loses his life for My sake will find it."**

Here was a man who denied himself. He didn't do what was best for him; he did what was best for his wife and his son. They needed him. The arrangement that had worked for so many years was no longer working. It was time for a new plan. So he walked away from his ministry success and mentored his son.

If he hadn't paid the price, he possibly could have lost his son.

And he couldn't take that risk.

So he denied himself, took up the cross of discipleship, embraced a smaller ministry and began to use the next twenty-four months to turn his boy into a man.

In doing so, he lost something. In a sense, he lost his life. He lost the crowds, the joy, and the privilege of seeing God change so many people's lives. But he had a son whose life needed some changes. And he needed a father to show him what those changes would be.

ANOTHER WAKE-UP CALL

About six years ago, I got my own wake-up call. It didn't come over the phone. It came from my own son. And it came right out of the blue. My then sixteen-year-old son was in trouble, and I had not realized it. Sure, he had shown the signs of any typical young man going through the throes of growing up. We had always been close, and I thought that I was on top of those things with him. But at the time when he needed me most, I suddenly woke up to a very hard truth. I had dropped the ball. I went through a fathering crisis that brought me to my knees and taught me some of the hardest lessons of this book. And I intend to share some of that crisis with you in the upcoming chapters. Suffice it to say that it was probably the most difficult crisis of my life. I found myself in over my head and nearly without hope.

We live out in the country, and it has been my habit for several years to take long walks, just to get away and think and pray. On those walks there are no phone calls or fax machines or interruptions...just me and the Lord and our two faithful retrievers, panting along by my side. During this crisis, those walks became my lifeline. I found myself crying out to God for help, praying for my son, for wisdom, for a breakthrough, throwing myself upon His mercy and promises.

And I want you to know that God has been faithful. He has kept his promise in Psalm 50:15, "Call upon Me in the day of trouble; I shall rescue you, and you will honor Me." By his goodness and grace he did rescue me in the time of trouble.

Are you in a place of trouble with one of your children? Your heavenly Father sees you and hears your cries. And he promises to be your Mentor and walk you through it. Just like he did for James Dobson Sr. And just as he has done for fathers down through the centuries.

THE TRIED-AND-TRUE METHOD

Fathering may be the single greatest challenge of your life. Especially if you didn't have a dad who showed you the way.

But take heart. God has given us a guide map, an instruction manual, a tried-and-true method. What he asks of you is that you accept the challenge and trust him to lead you.

It is your responsibility and no one else's. You alone can prepare your son to be a man and to take his place as the leader of the family tribe.

Don't let that responsibility fall on your wife. Mothers are important. But if you let your wife become the primary mentor of your sons, one of two things will end up happening. They will grow up to be feminized men, or they will grow up to be angry men. God calls upon fathers to mentor their sons.

These are hard times for young men. The messages around them are confusing and devastating. We can't depend on teachers or coaches or youth leaders to mentor our sons. It simply isn't enough. Your sons need you now more than ever.

This is a book about fathers mentoring sons. But let me give you a heads-up about what this book is not. It is not primarily a book on male or child psychology. Psychology is at its best when it is kneeling before the Word of God. This book is also not a formula for "how to make your son turn out okay," even though every father wants his son to turn out okay. Let me explain what I mean.

There are no perfect fathers so don't feel pressured to be one. There are no perfect prescriptions for fathering in this book or in any other. Fathers and sons are people. Fathers make mistakes. Sons make decisions. In fathering, we don't stick in a dollar (it used to be a quarter) and get out an ice-cold Coke. Fathering is more like building a house. You draw up the plans, you gather the materials, and then you start in. And you do the best job you can. Along the way, you might hit rock when you're digging the foundation, or lumber prices may rise, or it may rain for six straight months. Then the concrete drivers may go on strike. Inevitably, you will discover some adjustments you need to make that you hadn't foreseen in your original plans. That's sort of what fathering is like.

Fathers are sons that have grown up. They are flawed human beings. And children are individuals—each one with unique needs and personalities. That's why fathering is always a "learn as you go" thing. That's why every day is a new day for fathers. Sometimes you think you know your son, and then you find that you don't. Sometimes influences or circumstances that are completely out of your control enter into a son's life and deeply affect or derail him. Sometimes you find yourself on your knees with no answers at all. Other times you find yourself right in the middle of the fight of your life for this son God has given to you.

We're going to use the tried-and-true method in this book. We're going to go back to the authoritative, living, relevant Word of God and try to discover the lessons there for fathers on mentoring our sons.

And the place we are going to start is with the kings of the Old Testament.

KINGS AND FATHERS

Why start there? you may ask. Weren't most of those guys lousy fathers? Yes they were. But as Yogi Berra once said, "You can see a lot by looking." All of the kings were fathers. Some of them were good kings (a few were even great kings) but lousy fathers. Most of them were bad kings and bad fathers. One of them was a good king who became a good father. Yet from their lives we can learn vivid lessons about what children need in a father. The kings teach us that *a good man cannot simply rely on his example* to meet the needs of his son. A godly example is a great gift to a son. But the kings teach us that a man must be *intentional* in his fathering.

The famous painter Pablo Picasso was entertaining in his home when one of the guests noticed that he had none of his paintings hanging in his home.

"Why is that, Pablo? Do you not appreciate your own pictures?"

"On the contrary," replied Picasso. "I enjoy them very much. It's just that I can't afford them."

Picasso couldn't afford his own paintings.

You can't afford to not intentionally mentor your son. The Old Testament kings were all wealthy men, but as a group, they didn't consider the high price of *not* mentoring their sons. It cost them and the nation dearly.

You may not be a king, but you are the designated king of your home. Your wife is the queen. And your children are the subjects. One day, your sons will step up to the throne and carry on the family heritage. Their decisions will affect generations upon generations to come. As we will see, what happened in the lives of the Old Testament kings is utterly relevant to fathers today.

WHAT EVERY SON WANTS

Every son wants to be mentored by his father. He wants to have a special place in his father's heart. He wants to respect and emulate him. Down deep, he wants to know his father and be as close to him as possible. S. D. Gilbert said it well: "It may be hard on some fathers not to have a son, but it is much harder on a boy not to have a father."

Timmy Smith felt somewhat distanced from his stepfather. Timmy's family knew what it was to go through hard times. At times his mom worked three jobs to provide for the family. Timmy's hero was not his stepfather; it was a baseball pitcher by the name of Tug McGraw. Young Timmy kept McGraw's baseball card taped on his bedroom wall. He loved to see Tug McGraw pitch on TV and he loved the way he challenged the batters from the pitcher's mound. Young Timmy thought Tug was the coolest guy he had ever seen.

When Timmy was eleven, he was looking through some boxes for some pictures for a school report. You can imagine how shocked he was when he came across his birth certificate and read that his real father was none other than Tug McGraw. He had no idea. But this began a search to get to know his real father. After many years, the father and son reconciled. And Timmy eventually changed his name to reflect who it was he really belonged to. Tug McGraw recently passed away from cancer. And by his side was his son. Although they had been separated for years, they were finally reunited.

The father, Tug McGraw, once famed for his athletic ability, died in the care of a son with whom he had been reunited.

His son, Tim McGraw, one of the biggest stars in country music, was finally connected with the man who had been his hero before he knew he was his father.

And to both men it was clear that what ultimately mattered was not the fame or the fortune. It was the priceless relationship between father and son.[1]

"KING ME"

I can remember as a boy playing checkers with my dad. And when I would finally maneuver one of my checkers to the other side of the board, I would look at my dad and say, "King me." And then he would put a checker on top of my checker and it looked like a crown. Suddenly my little checker had turned into a king, and as king, he could move any direction that I deemed necessary.

That's what every son is saying to his father. Whether you realize it or not, there's nothing more in life that he wants than for you to "king him." One day you will pass off the scene and he will assume your role as head of the family. It's your job to prepare him and get him ready for that day. The best leaders think far enough ahead to groom a replacement. That's what fathering is all about. It's mentoring and equipping your son to become a man who will assume the family leadership for the next generation. You have no higher calling in life. It is your God-given assignment. There is nothing nobler in all of life than to shape your son into a man.

The kings didn't do it.

But with God's help, we still can.

What a father says to his sons is not heard by

the world, but it will be heard by posterity.

—JEAN PAUL RICHTER

CHAPTER TWO

BUILDING SONS INTO MEN

THE LORD JESUS IS THE KING OF KINGS.

He's not called the Presidents of Presidents. He is the King of Kings.

I'm an American. I imagine you are too. Americans aren't big on kings. We got started by fighting off a king. We have an inbred resistance to kings.

When you study American history, you don't study kings. You study the presidents.

When you study the Bible, you don't study presidents. You study the kings.

This is a book for fathers who want to mentor their sons to the glory of the Kings of Kings. So we are going to have to fight off our resistance to the kings. Have you ever seen one of those real large Bibles in an old church? If that Bible weighs twenty pounds, about eight of those pounds are about the kings.

A large chunk of your Bible is about the kings. But other than a few of the big hitters, most of us know very little about them. It's like listing the American presidents. Everyone knows about George Washington and Abraham Lincoln. And if you really think hard, you might remember who the other two presidents on Mount Rushmore are (Thomas Jefferson and Theodore Roosevelt). After that, until we get up to our own lifetime, it gets pretty murky. We have had a total of forty-three presidents in the history of America up until today (December 2004).

Interestingly enough, there were forty-three kings of Judah and Israel in the Old Testament. And their lives, their decisions, and their behaviors take up almost two-thirds of the Old Testament. Yet I would venture to say that besides David's shameful and sordid affair with Bathsheba, and Solomon's seven hundred wives and concubines, most guys know next to nothing about them. We know that they had lots of weird names and that most of them screwed up. This disturbs us. And it disturbs us even more that the kings who didn't screw up seemed to have sons that did. How can somebody who walked with God as closely as some of these kings did, yet end up with such messed-up kids? Our tendency is to throw up our hands and pretty much dismiss any hope of learning something worthwhile from them.

But God put them there for a reason. He doesn't want us to just skip over them.

My big study Bible is almost two inches thick and it has print that I can actually still read. The publisher laid it out so that the New Testament has 405 pages. The Old Testament comes out to 1344 pages. 936 of those pages relate to the kings. That's nearly an inch out of my two-inch- thick Bible!

Think about this. With the exception of Job (who was actually a king-type, a ruler over his own large and influential family clan), every book from chapter 8 of 1 Samuel until the end of the Old Testament is either *about* the kings (1 and 2 Samuel, 1 and 2 Kings, 1 and 2 Chronicles), *written* by a king (Psalms—mostly written by David, Proverbs, Ecclesiastes, Song of Solomon—written by Solomon), *remembering the judgment* that came on the nation because of the kings (Ezra, Nehemiah, Esther, Daniel), or the *actual judgments* of the prophets spoken to or during the time of the kings (Isaiah, Jeremiah, Lamentations, Ezekiel, Hosea, Joel, Amos, Obadiah, Jonah, Micah, Nahum, Habakkuk, Zephaniah, Haggai, Zechariah, Malachi).

In other words, these kings were important.

The King of Kings put these guys in there on purpose.

FUTURE KINGS

For the last seven or eight years, I have been circling these kings like a bush pilot looking for a place to land in the wilderness of Alaska. These kings, just like Alaska, cover a lot of territory. Then one day I was studying through Deuteronomy. Now, the book of Deuteronomy comes *before* the kings. Deuteronomy is the fifth book in the Bible. And it was written by Moses just as the Israelites were about to cross over Jordon into Canaan. Deuteronomy contains all of God's instructions for his people as they were about to enter the Promised Land and form a nation that would glorify him.

Have you ever read something in the Bible that seems a little weird? I have, and I did. In this case, it had to do with the kings. It struck me as I was reading along in Deuteronomy 17 that God was giving instructions for kings. That was strange since *they had no king.* God was their king, and he spoke to them through his chosen prophets and leaders. But God knew that the day would come when the people would demand a human king. He knew that they would not be happy until they were like all the other nations who had kings. So around chapter 17 of Deuteronomy, God laid down some specific commandments for these future kings through Moses.

There are some Christians who claim that God doesn't know the future. They are called "open theists." They have a very small view of God and a very large view of man's ability to shape his own destiny. They think that the Bible is a Microsoft Word document. I am writing this book with Microsoft Word. It's a great program because I can edit, cut, paste, or delete to my heart's content. That's how some teachers treat the Bible. They think it's a Microsoft Word document. But it's not. It is *the* Word. You don't change it, cut it, or delete it. You bow before it. You're not over it—you're under it.

The Bible clearly teaches that God knows everything, including the future. God knows our thoughts even before we think them. He knows the decisions we will make. He knew before the foundation of the world that you would be born, and He knew whom you would marry. He didn't just know it; He ordained it. He knew that you would have a son, and that you would need to mentor that son. He is not surprised at your son's unique personality and challenges. Your son has been part of his plan since before time. And God knows what he needs, and what you need in order to mentor him. That kind of takes the pressure off, doesn't it?

In the same way, God knew what the kings would need. So he gave specific instructions for them, so that he could bless them. Let me give them to you in a nutshell:

- *The king was not to multiply horses for himself (v. 16).*
- *The king was not to multiply wives for himself, lest his heart turn away from God (v. 17).*
- *The king was not to greatly increase silver and gold for himself (v. 17).*

Unless the scroll of Deuteronomy had been tossed in a closet somewhere as was the case with the boy-King Josiah (2 Chronicles 34), the kings of Israel and Judah knew these commandments well.

BEFORE DEUTERONOMY 17

But here is the kicker. And this is important, guys.

Before Deuteronomy 17 comes Deuteronomy 6. Deuteronomy 6 was for *all* the men of Israel—fathers, leaders, and kings. Every man, every father, and especially every king (as an example to the nation) was to follow Deuteronomy 6. It was a matter of life and death, said Moses. Deuteronomy 6:5–7 contains a job description for fathers. And the life of the nation depended on their doing this job (Deuteronomy 5:29, 33).

Do you have a job description? Most guys do. When you take on a job, you are given a description of your responsibilities. My son Josh recently interviewed for a part-time job. The job description responsibilities covered close to two pages. I told him that the only part-time thing about that job was going to be the pay.

Every man in Israel was given a job description by the Lord. And guys could understand it because it only comprised two things. Just two.

Job # 1: Love God Deeply

The first job is found in verses 5–6:

"You shall love the Lord your God with all your heart and with your soul and with all your might. These words, which I am commanding you today, shall be on your heart."

Fathers were to love the Lord their God from deep down in their heart and soul. Heart, soul, and might—that basically means "with your whole being." It's a wholehearted love. Nothing held back. No other allegiances or gods.

When you love God like that, His commands matter to you. Men tend to be warriors, to be protectors and keepers of honor. Men will fight to the death when honor is at stake. And God was saying, "Be a man of character and honor. Keep these commands ever upon your hearts which I am about to lay down as a lifeline for your families." Now, a man who loves the Lord in such a wholehearted way and cherishes his commands will obey those commands without a second thought. Love for God and obedience to his commands are two sides of the same coin.

Jesus said, "If you love me, you will keep my commandments." God didn't want fathers to obey simply out of duty. He wanted them to obey because they desired to do it out of a genuine love for Him. Kids can tell the difference. Kids need dads who love the Lord unashamedly and wholeheartedly. And by virtue of their love for God, they love his words. That's pretty simple.

Job # 2: Teach Your Son Diligently

The second job is found in verse 7:

"You shall teach them diligently to your sons and shall talk of them when you sit in your house and when you walk by the way and when you lie down and when you rise up."

Fathers were to be present in the lives of their sons, and they were to be very intentional in their presence. In the day-to-day give-and-take, they were to mentor their sons by modeling and teaching the truth of God to them. And they were to do so "diligently"—also another word for "wholeheartedly."

What time did you get up this morning to milk the cows? Now maybe your grandfather did that, but you probably didn't. But back in Bible times it was the normal way of life. We don't do that anymore, but they did. And they did it with their sons.

Picture an Israelite father. If God's words were on his heart, he would be thinking about them through the day. It would be natural to talk to his sons about the Lord while milking the goats or digging a well. He would talk about other things during the course of the day as well. But if God was at the center of the man's life, his son could not miss it. In the course of daily life, as the fathers were with their sons, they were to instruct them and teach them about life. In other words, a son would learn how to be a man by observing his father. The father would mentor his son by being "with" his son. It was the father's job to turn his son into a man—a godly man who also loved God from his gut, a responsible man, a man who would take over the family in his place when he breathed his last breath.

That was God's command for every man in Israel. And that is His command for every man today. These two instructions are not cute, clever, or designed by God to be easily marketed. They are given by God to save our lives and enable us to walk in his favor.

There is no "new and improved" version to these commands. They have not been upgraded. They were perfect when they were given and they will be perfect for as long as men walk the earth. Now most men don't milk goats and dig wells with their sons anymore. Most men walk out the door and get in their cars and go to work. Does this change the job description? No, it doesn't. The job description is timeless. It is non-cultural. The way a son becomes a man has not changed. So what does that mean? It means that our lifestyle today presents new challenges for a father.

A guy was walking down the street enjoying the fall afternoon. He then noticed an older man struggling with a washing machine in the doorway of his home. He quickly ran over and began to help the older man. They shoved, pulled, and lifted for several minutes before stopping in frustration. They just weren't making any progress. The younger man said, "I had no idea it would be so difficult to get this into the house." The older man replied, "What do you mean get it in? I'm trying to get it out."

Now both of these men had the best of intentions. But they were working against each other. If a man isn't working with the Lord, he's going to be frustrated when it comes to mentoring his son. Especially in this day and age. Fathers and sons used to spend hours together. But those days are gone unless we seize our time and make sure that we are working with the Lord to build our sons into men.

When was the last time you and your son made sandals together? First of all, you had to kill a cow. You would eat some of the meat, cure the rest to make jerky, and save the hide. One of the things you used that hide for was sandals. You had to work the leather and get it to the right texture of softness that your feet would be comfortable with. Then you would cut the leather, sew it, reinforce it, and finally wear it. During that entire process, you and your son would be interacting. Not always talking, but always interacting. Fathers and sons did that for thousands of years. Now if you need sandals, you buy them at the mall or on the Internet.

It's going to require some thought and creativity and a certain amount of sacrifice to mentor our sons. And that's why we are going to spend some time thinking about that in this book. But we can be assured of this: God will provide a way for you to mentor when you take His Word seriously.

FLUNKING OUT

So what about the kings? Could they get off the hook by hiring someone to do these two tasks for them? The answer is no. The kings were not excluded from these foundational responsibilities. If anything, they were *doubly* responsible, because they were to be examples to the nation. So what was it that these kings were to do?

First, the kings were to love the Lord their God with all their heart, all their soul, and all their might (Deuteronomy 6:5). Second, they were to train and mentor their sons to replace them on the throne that they would one day vacate. They had to have enough vision to not only build their kingdoms but to build their sons so that they would be equipped to one day lead the kingdom in their absence.

This is the entire purpose of the book of Proverbs. It is written from a father to a son. When you read through Proverbs next time, note how many times the term "my son" is used. When I recently read through Proverbs, I found that phrase used twenty-three times in thirty-one chapters. Proverbs is a book from a king-father to a prince-son. It is a book in which a father is coaching and providing his son with wisdom for what he will surely face in life.

So that was the twofold assignment given to the kings. The question is, how did they do?

Last year I spent nine months going through a study of the kings with a group of guys in our church. Frankly, we were all surprised at just how much these kings were just like us. They may have driven Lexus chariots and had Rolex sundials, but these guys had the same basic issues as we have today. They struggled over sex and women. They had demanding schedules, money worries, and potential hostile takeovers. These potential hostile takeovers meant that you would lose not only your throne but your head. They had rebellious and spoiled kids who needed to be disciplined and mentored. They constantly thought about success, image, and a legacy of significance. And they tended to make the same mistakes we all make. All of them had lessons to teach us about raising sons.

But when it came down to writing a book on these kings, I realized I had a book series on my hands. It would be impossible to do justice to them all in one book. Let me just give you a taste:

- *Jereboam could have been a great king. But he was a control freak, and as a result he lost his legacy and his kingdom.*
- *Amaziah started out on a good path but couldn't handle godly input and counsel. So he died a sick and bitter old man.*
- *Ahab rebelled against God, then married the wrong woman, the infamous, ambitious, wicked Jezebel; then he punted his leadership to her,*

sealing his own fate and the fate of his children.

• *Jehoshaphat ruled well, until he gave his son in marriage to Ahab and Je-zebel's daughter, Athaliah. Before it was all over, Athaliah had usurped the throne, killed all her offspring (save only little Joash who was hidden away by God's grace), and annihilated the priesthood. There is no more vivid lesson on the need for biblical fathering than that of Jehoshaphat. By an impulsive, short-term decision he brought grief, violence, and murder to his family for generations.*

The list goes on, and the lessons are rich.

But like the bush pilot in the wilderness of Alaska, I finally had to settle down somewhere. Three kings in particular—David, Solomon, and his son Rehoboam—teach some of the most compelling lessons about biblical fathering. And so in this book, we will dwell on these three: David, the king who learned from his mistakes; Solomon, the wisest fool who ever lived; and Rehoboam, the guy who lost a kingdom in seventy-two hours. Stick these three in your pocket, and you have a mini-manual on fathering.

WHERE THE KINGS WENT WRONG

But before we leave the other forty kings behind, there are a few sweep-ing conclusions we can make about them. As a group that stretches over three hundred years, they failed miserably. Of the forty kings who reigned in Judah and Israel after Solomon, only eight were considered "good."

Generally speaking, the kings as a group (with a few notable excep-tions):

• *Bankrupted their souls instead of loving the Lord.*

They watched over their real estate, their palaces, their armies, and their accounts receivables, but they didn't watch over their souls. The prophet Jeremiah nails them when he says to God: "You are near to their lips but far from their mind" (Jeremiah 12:2).

They watched over everything that seemed to matter, but they didn't love him, know him, or follow him. That's what really matters for eternity, but they were short-term, impulsive investors with their souls.

Thus says the Lord, "Let not a wise man boast of his wisdom, and let not the mighty man boast of his might, let not a rich man boast of his riches; but let him who boasts boast of this, that he understands and knows Me, that I am the Lord who exercises lovingkindness, justice and righteousness on the earth; for I delight in these things," declares the Lord. (JEREMIAH 9:23–24)

Across the board of the generations, with a handful of notable exceptions, these kings boasted about everything that didn't matter. That's why most of these guys were full of hot air. They were small potatoes, self-centered men who didn't have the vision to think beyond themselves. When it came to thinking about their sons, they flunked out.

As a result, they:

• *Built kingdoms instead of sons.*

It was common for the kings at a certain point to promote their sons and establish a co-regency. The co-regency wasn't a hotel. It was sort of an apprentice program for the son who would take over the throne upon his father's death. He would learn the ropes about ruling as he showed up for work every day with his father. He would learn how to deal with domestic issues as well as the big stuff of international affairs. But just because a king co-ruled with his son didn't mean that he connected with his son.

HARDWIRED TO CONNECT

I experienced a severe personal disappointment last week. I couldn't watch football over Thanksgiving weekend. And it was all due to a wrong connection. Since we are out in the country, my only access to football is through my small satellite dish. I had some kind of glitch and the repairman came out to fix the problem. But he created another when he failed to correctly connect the wire that runs between the TV and the receiver. In other words, he screwed up on the hardwiring. And I'll go ahead and confess it now. I wasn't real thankful about the situation.

Hardwired has become a familiar term to our culture.

Webster says, "hardwired: 1. Having a direct physical connection, such as by wire or cable."

Fathers and sons are to have a hardwired connection. That is God's plan. The enemy is working overtime to sever that connection. And unfortunately, he's having much success. I recently came across a study that underscored the problem.

The study is titled "Hardwired to Connect: The New Scientific Case for Authoritative Communities." The study was conducted by Dartmouth Medical School, the Institute for American Values, and the YMCA of America. They should have titled it "Why What God Says to Fathers Is True."

I read the entire study. One thing that stood out to me was that in an age of remarkable prosperity, more and more children are suffering from depression, anxiety, and substance abuse.[1] Why is that? They aren't connected to a loving, caring authority figure who will discipline them when necessary. In fact, they aren't connected at all. "The idea," says Allan N. Schore of the UCLA School of Medicine, "is that we are born to form attachments, that our brains are physically wired to develop in tandem with another's, through emotional communication, beginning before words are spoken."[2]

God has hardwired us from the womb. And he has hardwired us for relationships. And one of those relationships is a father and his children. Kids in America are in trouble because many of them have lost this central connection to their dads. They've got a dish, a receiver, and a TV. But somehow the wiring has gotten messed up and they are not getting a clear picture. They are getting clothes, money, and cars, but they are not getting what they need. That's why they are so depressed and confused. They are not wired into Dad. Dad's too busy building his kingdom to build into them.

I found it interesting that this secular report is underscoring almost everything that God said to the men of Israel in Deuteronomy 6. You don't expect that to come out of the academic world these days. But things have so broken down in our culture that people are becoming desperate—so desperate that they are willing to tell the truth.

The subtitle of this report contains the word *authoritative*. For many in our culture, and especially in academia, anything "authoritative" is bad. So the authors had to explain themselves so that people who react to "authority" would keep reading. I quote the two paragraphs for a reason, as you shall see:

> Our choice of the word "authoritative" comes after considerable reflection, especially since we are concerned that readers of this report, and members of the public who may hear about it, might

confuse "authoritative" with "authoritarian," a word which is commonly associated with a largely coercive ("command and control") approach to raising children and relating to others. We are eager to avoid that confusion. But we believe that the word *authoritative* is worth reclaiming and using.

First the word refers to a strong body of scholarly evidence demonstrating the value of that particular *combination of warmth and structure* in which children in a democratic society appear most likely to thrive. Second, the word comes from the Latin *auctor*, which can mean "one who creates." We like that. Authoritative communities don't just happen. They are created and sustained by dedicated individuals with a shared vision of building a good life for the next generation.[3]

Did you catch that? This report is saying that children need a community of both *authority*—the kind of biblical authority which combines structure and warmth—and *connection*. Now let met ask you something. To whom does God give the responsibility for such authority in the home? He gives it to husbands and fathers (Ephesians 5 and 6, Colossians 3, 1 Timothy 3). And what does he command a father to do in Deuteronomy 6? He commands him to connect with his children. This report is saying in essence that children today have a desperate need for biblical fathering. While it doesn't say it this way, that is precisely what it is saying. And why is that true? Because the Ultimate One who created mankind set it up this way. A father's authority and connection with his children are so important to the survival of a nation that it is commanded by God in Deuteronomy, and reiterated time and again throughout Scripture.

WHEN AUTHORITY BREAKS DOWN

Our nation has set aside the authority of God. And there are tremendous consequences to doing so. When the authority of God is rejected, sons and daughters get hurt. Here is the statement of a twenty-seven-year-old young man who reflects back on an upbringing without authority. You will see that his mother was divorced, remarried, and then embraced lesbianism. This young man is deeply hurt and confused, all because he was raised in a home without biblical authority.

> Lesbians should not fill their children with their own fears and hatreds. I say this after considering the causes of needless pain in my past, and my troubles understanding the present.... I do recall our wishing our mothers were more attentive to us than to each other. We kids would get together and have sex, males or females in any combination—unbeknownst to our parents, but ironically I don't think any of us really knew what our mothers' lesbianism really meant.... Since my parents had sex with the same sex (my mother with other women, my stepfather with me), I had not understood that homosexuality was wrong. Also, at the time I couldn't figure out my own sexuality because I was having sex with people of both sexes.[4]

I grant you this is an extreme situation. Quite frankly, it is an unthinkable situation for a child to be raised in. But when the authority of God is rejected, then marriage is rejected, homosexual marriage is approved, and children get devastated.

This report is quite good. It is also very sad. It concludes that there is a horrific crisis taking place among even the most affluent children in

America. Josh McDowell bottom-lines the finding of the report: "What's causing this crisis of American childhood is a lack of connectedness— close connections to other people and deep connections to moral and spiritual meaning." [5]

I would summarize the report this way: The instructions that God gave to fathers in Deuteronomy 6 are not being fulfilled by fathers.

Fathers are too busy. Fathers are supposed to be busy. But it's easy to get so busy making money that we are losing connection with our sons. You might be thinking, *But I have daughters*. Well, I have a daughter, too, and I love her with all of my heart. But this isn't a book about daughters. It's a book about sons. Who is your daughter going to marry? Can I tell you what I hear from my twenty-five-year old daughter and her Christian friends on a regular basis? They tell me that the Christian guys as a whole aren't much different from the non-Christian guys. Now here and there you will find outstanding exceptions to that. But as a whole, these young Christian guys have not been mentored. And many of them at twenty-five are so ill-equipped and unprepared for life that they are scared to death to make a commitment.

These young men should be eating commitment for breakfast. They should be chomping at the bit to assume responsibility for a wife and children and to build a godly heritage. But half of these guys are still playing video games. They don't have a clue what it means to be a godly man because their fathers didn't do the job. They may have given them cars and seven irons and trips to Europe, but they didn't give them what counts. Are your boys still under your roof? Then understand this. They don't need more things. They need you. They need for you to give them Deuteronomy 6.

A CRISIS AMONG BOYS

When boys don't connect with their dads, bad things happen to them. Real bad things.

"In the midst of unprecedented material affluence, large and growing numbers of U.S. children and adolescents are failing to flourish. . . . More and more young people are suffering from mental illness, emotional distress, and behavioral problems."[6]

Those are bad things.

Primarily, it is the boys who are in trouble. And they are in trouble because they aren't being mentored. Dr. Dobson has recently discovered some tragic news about the state of boys when compared with girls: They are

- *six times more likely to have learning disabilities,*
- *three times more likely to be registered drug addicts,*
- *four times more likely to be diagnosed as emotionally disturbed,*
- *twelve times more likely to murder, and*
- *50 percent more likely to die in a car accident.*[7]

And that's not all:

- *Boys younger than fifteen years of age are twice as likely to be admitted to psychiatric hospitals.*
- *Boys younger than fifteen are five times more likely than girls to kill themselves.*
- *Boys comprise 90 percent of those in drug treatment programs.*
- *Boys represent 95 percent of the cases in juvenile court.*[8]

Dr. Dobson summarizes the tragic situation when he writes:

"Now, more than ever, boys are experiencing a crisis of confidence that reaches deep within the soul. Many of them are growing up believing they are unloved by their parents and are hated or disrespected by their peers."[9]

That is an unspeakable tragedy.

I received the following letter several weeks ago. I will include it unsigned and without any corrections to the spelling or grammar. As you will see, there are much larger issues here than punctuation:

> *Dear Steve Farrar,*
>
> *Hey, I am just writing to tell you how much your book is helping get my life towards the Lord. In my current situation, I'm in a bit of a bind. I'm 17 years of age, in jail waiting to be tried for Capitol Murder. No I didn't kill anybody if that what your thinking. I just followed the wrong people who ended up robbing a store and taking one men's life. I've had a hard life, no one to care for me. All my history is with Child Protective Services. My mom chose boyfriends over me so I hit the streets living with friends and ended up in here. While I was in here I found I have a little boy born 2 moths age. That is one of the reason I am turning my life around, to give that child what I never had. The other is without the lord I'm without hope. Your book has taught me a lot and want to thank you as well. I would like to hear from you. I'll be her. Sadly. Well Thanks for your time.*

Here is a boy in trouble because he has no father—just a series of boyfriends in his mother's life. And now he's a father at seventeen, facing the rest of his life in prison.

Do you have a son? Where is he right now? What is he doing? Who is he with? When was the last time you had some significant time and significant conversation with him? I know you're busy. But he is your son. Tell me, what is more important than pouring your life into him as the Lord Jesus poured his life into the disciples?

Boys need their dads. They need their dads to do stuff with them and put them to bed. They need dads who will discipline them when they cross the line. They need dads who love Christ and follow him. They need dads who don't lie, don't cheat, and don't look at porn. They need dads that love their mothers and don't cut out when the going gets tough. They need dads who won't put up with disrespectful words or looks aimed at Mom. They need dads who can tell them how to handle a bully at school. And if need be, they need a dad who will go talk to the father of the bully or bullies. And if the bully has no father, they will talk to the mother. And if the father or mother of the bully won't do anything, then your son needs a dad who will model how to put the fear of God in the bully.

A dad like that can talk to his boys about God and the truth of the Scriptures. They may not act like they're listening, but they are. And more importantly, they are watching. What are they watching for? They are watching to see if you really believe what you say. If you believe it, you will live it. They will love you, respect you, and want to grow up and be like you. Not all of the time, but the vast majority of the time. They may have times of rebellion and hardness of heart, but in the end, the vast majority of kids raised by fathers like that are going to come around full circle and wind up teaching their kids the principles of Deuteronomy 6.

The report doesn't say it in those words, but they are sure coming close. And whether they say it or not is irrelevant. God says it.

With a few exceptions, the kings of Israel and Judah didn't do that. They were building their net worth and their kingdoms instead of their sons. And it led to the spiritual bankruptcy of both nations.

BUILDING 170 BRIDGES

You've heard of the Panama Canal. But long before there was a Panama Canal there was a Panama Railroad. A case could be made that it was the most difficult railroad built anywhere at any time. Built in 1850 at the height of the California gold rush, it was

> the first ocean-to-ocean railroad, its completion predating that of the Union Pacific by fourteen years. Mile for mile it also appears to have cost more in dollars and in human life than any railroad ever built.... The surveys made by its builders produced important geographic revelations that had a direct bearing on the decision to build a Panama canal along the same route.... Still, the simple fact that it was built remains the overriding wonder, given the astonishing difficulties that had to be overcome and the means at hand in the 1850s. Present-day engineers who had experience in jungle construction wonder how in the world it was ever managed.... It is almost inconceivable... that the railroad survey—just the survey—could have been made by a comparative handful of men who had no proper equipment for topographic reconnaissance (no helicopters, no recourse to aerial photography), no modern medicines, nor the least understanding of the causes of malaria or yellow fever. There was no such thing as an insect repellent, no bulldozers, no chain saws, no canned goods, not one reliable map....
>
> The original line was five-foot, or broad, gauge, and it was built as hurriedly and cheaply as circumstances would allow.... Still, this one little stretch of track took nearly five years to build and cost $8 million, which averages out to a little less than ten miles a year and a then unheard-of $168,000 per mile.
>
> Part of the construction problem can be appreciated in a single

statistic. In those forty-seven and a half miles it was necessary to build 170 bridges of more than twelve feet each in length.[10]

That's what it is like to mentor a son. Every time you turn around, you are going to have to build another bridge. Bridges cost. They cost money and time. And the bridges that you build with your son at the age of seven are not going to cut it when he's twenty-seven. At twenty-seven, he's facing bigger mountains than he has ever seen in his entire life, and it's still your job to be hanging around as a consultant so that he can successfully keep charging ahead. He's never been twenty-seven before. You have. And what a benefit it is to talk with someone who has been over the bridge just before you step onto it.

That's fathering and that is mentoring.

That's my job and yours.

What does your son need? He needs you to love the Lord from your gut, and then he needs for you to mentor him. He knows that one day it will all be on his shoulders, and he desperately wants to know that he can handle it. In a recent note to me, one of my sons, now in his twenties, expressed the fears that every son feels, and with his permission, I share it here with you:

> *There are a few things in my life that I fear greatly. They are mostly inevitable times that I know I must live through in this short life on earth. One of them is the day I get married, mainly because of the huge responsibility that will put on me as a husband. Another one is the day that I have my first child, for many reasons that I need not explain. But while these are times of new responsibility in a man's life, they are more of a time of joy*

because family is a blessing from the Lord and I look forward to that.

But the day that I fear the most above all else is the day of your death. It scares me to think of life without you. In the past it has scared me to the point that I couldn't even think about it. But I now realize that while I will lose my earthly father, my heavenly father will always be there for me. To do all that you have done for me and so much more. And he is already starting to take over that role.

My death is inevitable.

Your death is inevitable.

The kings of the Old Testament are dead.

The fathers that have gone before us are dead.

Someday you and I will breathe our last and pass on the mantle.

So who is going to take over the leadership of your family when you depart this earthly real estate? As the kings of Israel and Judah sat on their golden thrones, apparently they didn't give that a whole lot of thought.

But you say, "My kids aren't small anymore. They're away at college or they are married with kids of their own." That may be so, but you are still their father. Bridges can be built at any stage of life. And is it not true that young men can learn valuable lessons from older men? If your son is twenty-seven, then he's facing issues that could overwhelm him. He could use your wise and respectful counsel because you are still his dad. And you still love him.

Most men are overwhelmed at the challenge of building a son. That's why they're not doing it. It takes everything you have. It's as hard as cutting a railroad through the jungles of the Panama mountains.

But the One who made the mountains will navigate you through.

You will have days when you're stuck and you are confused and you don't know what the heck you're doing. I know, because I've been there.

But here's the good news.

You have a Father who is connected with you. He's got his eye on you. He knows what you're up against. If your son is struggling, he knows your heartache. If you feel like you've been a failure, he can give you the concrete you need to start building some bridges. If you don't know what to do today, he will make a way and show you. He will lead you through. Not around, not above, but through. He won't leave you and he won't abandon you. And he wants you to succeed.

You've got a Father.

That's why you can father.

You're not in this by yourself.

It's not the tragedies that kill us, it's the messes.

—DOROTHY PARKER

3

RAPID RESPONSE

(MENTORING THROUGH MISTAKES)

WE ALL KNOW WHAT DAVID DID WRONG.

But David also did some things right.

Yes, he did commit adultery with Bathsheba, and yes, he did arrange for her husband to be killed in combat. And yes, he attempted to cover up his sin by marrying Bathsheba and living a lie and hiding his bloody sin for nearly a year. He was manufacturing the impression that he was a man of honor by marrying the pregnant wife of one of his fallen soldiers. But David had seduced the man's wife while Uriah was away from home fighting for David. And then, after David had gotten the man's wife pregnant, he arranged for Uriah to come home and have some time with his wife. Uriah was so honorable that he wouldn't sleep with his wife if his men couldn't be with their wives. So David had him set up and murdered (2 Samuel 11).

That's what David did wrong.

But when Nathan the prophet confronted him, David broke,

and he came clean about his sin. He retched over his sin with the
dry heaves of genuine repentance and threw himself on the mercy
of God.

David knew what it was to sin.

And I know it and you know it.

That was a terrible chapter in David's life. But in the mercy of
God, he gives broken men the opportunity to write new chapters in
their lives. After screwing up his integrity, his character, and his reputation, David was determined to do some things right with the rest of
his life. He continued to deal with the consequences of his adultery
and murder in his own family for the rest of his life. There is a tremendous cost to sin.

Maybe that's where you are. You are sick of your sin and there's
no one to blame for the mess that you're in except for yourself. As you
turn to Christ and give him every ounce of your life and heart, he can
enable you to start getting some things right. It's not too late. It really
isn't.

TWO TOWERING SHOTS

As a matter of fact, David did a lot of things right. Two things immediately come to mind that David did right.

   1. *David was a man after God's own heart.*

   2. *David was the only king who attempted to biblically mentor his son.*

Those were two towering home runs that David put out of the
ballpark. And you will notice that number one and number two fulfill
the job description that God gave to every man and king out of Deuteronomy 6.

First, David loved the Lord and followed him from his heart of hearts. When Samuel was sent to anoint him as king, the Lord told Samuel that "man looks at the outward appearance, but the Lord looks at the heart" (1 Samuel 16:7). David was chosen because of his heart. After he died, it was said of David that he was "a man after God's own heart," and that his heart was "wholly devoted to the Lord" (1 Kings 11:4).

When you think about all of David's sins and blunders, that is a remarkable statement. It's a very redeeming statement, because it tells us that when we genuinely repent, the Lord is merciful to cleanse us and to bless and use us. Did David therefore escape the consequences of his sin? Absolutely not. All of his days he endured one pain upon another as a result of his poor decisions. But he never turned bitter and blamed God. In the end, he loved the Lord with a whole heart and as we will see, he did learn through his ghastly mistakes.

Did David follow the Lord perfectly? No. And neither do I. You don't either. But God is not looking for perfection—he's looking at your heart. And if you are loving him from the deepest part of your heart and soul, *there is going to be a growing consistency in your walk.* I think it was Tommy Nelson who said you never become sinless, but you will begin to sin less. That's a big lesson we can learn from David.

Second, David attempted to mentor and prepare Solomon to assume the leadership of the nation for the next generation. I want to state this one more time for the record. As far as I can determine from my reading of all the kings, I don't see any other king who purposefully tried to prepare and mentor his son before the Lord, other than David. I'm sure that many of the other kings made sure that their sons were educated in all of the intricacies of kingsmanship. But I don't see that any of them attempted to mentor them with a heart for the Lord the way that David did with Solomon. There may have been others, but if there were, their efforts to mentor are not clearly recorded.

David was a complete and total failure as a father to his other sons. He knew that in his heart. He was reminded of it every day. But he wasn't going to make the same mistakes again. He was going to try and get it right with Solomon. That's why we have to give David an A for effort when it came to mentoring Solomon.

EARLY MISTAKES

David had a bunch of sons from a bunch of different wives—which he had no business in doing. He should have obeyed Deuteronomy 17:17 and been married to one wife. But I can't get into that here. I have covered that issue of David's life in my book *Finishing Strong*, and you can study that further if you so desire.

My point is this. David had some other sons that he had not mentored before the Lord as he did with Solomon. Three of them were absolute wrecks: Amnon, Absalom, and Adonijah. And the wretched story of their lives is found in 2 Samuel 12–24 and 1 Kings 1–2. But what follows in the next paragraph is the short version.

Amnon raped his half-sister Tamar. David chose not to discipline Amnon. In response to that, Absalom waited two years for his chance and then murdered Amnon for the rape of Tamar. David chose to discipline Absalom, but he unwisely built no bridges with this son. He removed Absalom and simply put him in the corner. Absalom would later nearly pull off a palace coup and take the throne from his father. David actually had to flee Jerusalem for his life, and when he left Jerusalem, Absalom had sex in public with David's concubines to humiliate his father. One of David's generals, Joab, eventually killed Absalom, and the grieving David then returned to his throne in Jerusalem. Later, when David was on his deathbed, his son Adonijah attempted to take the throne without his father's approval, and to steal it from Solomon, his yet-to-be crowned half brother. Even in death, David had to deal with a rebellious and self-centered son.

These boys all grew up with wealth and privilege. They drove new chariots and went to the best schools. They wore the right clothes and the right shoes. They had all the spending money that they needed. David saw to it that every material need and want was provided for his sons. But what a hellhole that palace must have been. Alexander Whyte, the great Scottish preacher, describes so vividly what David had created:

> David's palace was a perfect pandemonium of suspicion, and intrigue, and jealousy, and hatred—all breaking out, now into incest and now into murder. And it was into such a household, if such a cesspool could be called a household, that Absalom, David's third son by his third living wife, was born and brought up. . . .
>
> A little ring of jealous and scheming parasites, all hateful and hating one another, collected round each one of David's wives. And it was in one of the worst of the wicked little rings that Absalom grew up and got his education.
>
> "The inconceivable evil of sensuality" was surely never more awfully burned in upon any sinful house than it was upon David's house.[1]

All of his boys grew up in that wealthy cesspool. A cesspool of David's own making. David had many wives and he had many sons.

As I have reread the accounts of David's life, it becomes very clear that David was not a model father. He didn't discipline his sons (1 Kings 1:6), and his own example of sexual sin and murder had to surely undercut his ability to build character into their lives. His three difficult sons each belonged to a different wife, and that very fact bred distrust and jealousy among them.

But he paid dearly for the consequences of his sins of adultery and murder in his own home. When a man's children are involved in incest, murder, and betrayal over a period of years, it's safe to say that David had a broken heart over what he had set into motion.

He certainly never wanted to be that kind of father. That was never his intention. But life sort of snuck up on him. Before he knew it he had so much responsibility that he couldn't see straight. He had cabinet meetings, military meetings, internal bickering among his staff, budget issues, wife issues (at least eight wives with all of their individual issues), and homeland defense issues. Every time David looked up he had someone wanting something from him. He couldn't get a moment to himself. And in the midst of all this responsibility, he let his fathering slowly fall by the wayside. Oh sure, he paid the bills, showed up at their games, and hired the tutors. But fathering is much more than that. He knew that, but with everything else going on, he got seriously distracted.

The counsel of C. H. Spurgeon is to be heard when it comes to David: "It would be wise to sympathize as far as we can, than to sit in judgment upon a case which has never been our own."[2]

An episode of serious distraction happens to every man at one point or another. And in the course of your life, it may happen more than once. For some guys, it's a permanent condition. But that's not what you want. We love our sons and we would do anything for them. We would die for them. But sometimes we get pulled away from fathering them in the areas that they need it the most. Only a father can teach his son to be a man. We get caught up in our careers and providing. We are trying to give them what we never had. We don't want to them to go without. And in all that good motivation, it's possible to get distracted and not give them what they must have. What your son needs is you.

ONE LAST SHOT

David had blown it with his other sons, but he had one more shot with Solomon. How old was Solomon at this point? We don't know, but David said his son was "young and inexperienced" (1 Chronicles 22:5; 29:1).[3] So we don't know Solomon's chronological age—we just know he still needed his father to step up to the plate in order to mentor and coach him.

When Solomon was still young and inexperienced, David began to pour his energies into mentoring and preparing Solomon to follow him on the throne. He knew that he had screwed up as a father. He had failed to do the job with his other sons. But in the final chapters of his life, David would pour all of his energies into fathering and mentoring Solomon to take the leadership mantle into the next generation.

If David was anything, he was a fighter. He wasn't a quitter. It wasn't in his nature to sit passively by and let everything in his home continue to fall apart.

So he made a major midcourse correction.

He decided that it was time for him to start mentoring and stop being a passive, distant, and absent father. It was time to build a son. It was time to give his son what he really needed.

Just like David, you, too, can make a midcourse correction. No matter what your situation, your age, the sins of your past—David teaches us that it is never too late to change course. You can still become the father your son desperately needs.

In fact, it is here that you cannot fail.

The Enemy will do everything, absolutely everything in his power to distract you so that you will fail.

You cannot let that happen.

MAN STUFF

Last week I was having lunch with my son John. John was home for a few days from college in California. He will graduate in six months and then will return to Texas to begin his career as a firefighter. After a quick lunch, he asked me to drive him by the city fire department so he could pick up information on the fire academy. As I watched him walk into the fire station, I was surprised when I got tears in my eyes. I had some trouble fighting them off. But I didn't fight too hard because these were good tears.

They were tears of gratefulness to the Lord. At this point in his life, John could not be doing any better. He is walking with the Lord and he has clear purpose and goals. He will graduate on time with a degree in physical education and a minor in Bible. He is mentoring six junior high boys at his church.

But that's not where he was six years ago. He was in trouble and was showing all of the symptoms. But I wasn't picking up on it. I am telling you this episode in our lives with John's permission. He has read this and given it the green light. It's important that you know that. It's also important that you understand the main point of what you are about to read. The point is not that John got himself into trouble. The point is that it happened right under my nose and I didn't see it. That's the point. This is about where I came up seriously short. I screwed up.

John was making some bad decisions that resulted in some bad friends. And then that resulted in drinking, partying, and some drugs. But John was smart, and he was smart enough to keep this away from the house. I have to confess that I thought I was pretty savvy. But he conned me for a number of months.

Then one night during a brief conversation he said something that hit my radar screen. I can't even remember what he said, but whatever it was, I knew he was hiding something from me. Something major. And I didn't know what it was. I just knew he was in trouble.

So I started fasting and praying every Tuesday. Instead of eating meals, I would take the time normally devoted to meals and I would go off by myself and I would pray for John. I asked the Lord to let me know what it was that was going on in his life. There was something there but I didn't know what. And if I just confronted him, it wasn't going to work. It needed to come from him. So I asked the Lord to work in such a way that John would come to me and tell me what he was up to. About six weeks later, God answered that prayer.

It was completely unexpected. One evening right after dinner, Mary, John, and I were sitting in the living room. I had just turned on a basketball game. Mary was drinking a cup of coffee and everything was very normal. And then suddenly we were into it. John said something that got my attention. I turned off the TV and asked him a question and then he started to break. He began to tell me that he had made a lot of bad decisions that he had been hiding from me and that he was in trouble and didn't know how to get out of it.

Here's this big weight lifting kid with heaviness on his shoulders and tears rolling down his cheeks. I went over to him and knelt down beside the chair and put my arm around him.

"John, I want to help you but I can't until I know what kind of trouble you're in."

"I can't tell you, Dad. I'm too ashamed. I've let you and Mom down."

"If you're in trouble, and I don't know what it is, then I've let you down," I said. "But whatever it is that you're in, we'll walk through it together.

"So John, I'm going to ask you some questions. And you just tell me yes or no. Are you drinking?"

He nodded yes.

"Are you getting drunk?" "Yes."

"Are you smoking marijuana?" "Yes."

"Have you tried other stuff?" "Yes."

"What else have you tried?" I asked as I braced myself for the worst.

Thankfully, John had not gone as far down the road as I had feared. But he had definitely gotten on the wrong path.

You can imagine that it was quite a scene in the living room. God had given us the start of a breakthrough. John was pouring out his heart and telling us about what he had gotten himself into. He knew what he was doing was wrong. But he didn't know if he could talk to God about it. In fact, he wasn't even sure there was a God. I was listening to all this in shock and stunned disbelief. Sure, I knew that John's grades were down and that he was terribly disappointed over some setbacks he had in sports. Those "broken dreams" in basketball had devastated him. I knew that. But I was stunned by what I was hearing.

BLINDSIDED

We had never had an ounce of rebellion during our children's teenage years. And John had always been a happy kid who loved the Lord and everyone around him. But over the previous months, he had been developing a hard heart. I knew that, but I couldn't believe how quickly he had spiraled downward. I couldn't believe how confused he was.

And then I remembered that just months before, I had written a chapter for a new book. I had titled the chapter "Confused Christian Kids." I wrote that chapter for other men. Now I had one under my roof and didn't even know it. That's how distracted I had become. We had always been close, very close. John would tell you that. We talked about everything. But very gradually, I started to lose touch with John's heart. I don't know quite how that happened, but it did.

I would like to tell you that everything got fixed that evening. But it didn't. This all came out just a few days before Thanksgiving. And I was very thankful that I didn't have any conferences until the middle of January. I will tell you this—it was the most difficult, heartbreaking holiday time we've ever had as a family. It was hell on earth as we attempted to sort out the difficulty in our home. Mary and I were divided over how we should handle the situation with John. I've got a great wife and she would die for our kids just as I would. And we have always attempted to present a united front to our kids. But we had a son who was in a deep pit, and we had to rescue him, and we found that we had different ideas as to how we could best bring him out.

Suddenly, we had a conflict on two fronts—with our son and with each other. It was a gut-wrenching time. And I'm the guy who's supposed to have the answers because I write books to men. I didn't know snot. I had lost every ounce of wisdom that I thought I ever had.

And then I remembered a section I had written in my first book, *Point Man*. Of course, I had written it to other men back in 1990:

> It is abundantly clear that one of the goals of the enemy is to interrupt this link of biblical families from generation to generation. He does this by implementing two strategies:
>
> **Strategy #1:** *To effectively alienate and sever a husband's relationship with his wife.*
>
> **Strategy #2:** *To effectively alienate and sever a father's relationship with his children.*[4]

It was clear that my family was under attack. The Enemy was attempting to alienate me from my son and in the process was trying to alienate me from Mary. This was an in-your-face, full frontal assault on my family. This was a war. And I was feeling very defeated. I was ready to resign from my ministry. I was ready to stop speaking. And I would have if there had not been a breakthrough from the Lord.

The first breakthrough came between Mary and John. She was able to go to him and seek his forgiveness, just as had happened between John and me. And their relationship was healed.

The second breakthrough came where Mary and I had been divided. We each began to understand where the other was coming from—both of us had something valuable to contribute in this tough situation. Together we sought the counsel of a few trusted friends, some of whom had gone through the same experience with a child. We needed to know what steps to take with John. We needed the next step. And that was the next breakthrough. The steps began to become clear. With a united front, we began to take those steps, all the while throwing ourselves on the mercy of God.

WALKING THROUGH THE PROCESS

I need to be very clear here. Everything didn't get fixed overnight. For John, it actually was a process that took several years. But the process had started and we could see that God was at work.

Another breakthrough was when John decided to walk away from the stimulants and the friends. Leaving his friends was by far the hardest choice. He knew that he would find himself virtually alone and ostracized by the crowd. And guess what. They did ostracize him. And he was lonely. It was the hardest thing he ever did, but he did it.

With each of these breakthroughs, only moments before it had seemed hopeless. But then God intervened and did an unexpected work.

Could I have orchestrated these breakthroughs? No. I could only stay on my knees and stay in the fight for both my wife and my son. The rest was up to the Lord. I was utterly at his mercy. And he was utterly gracious.

You may be wondering about the steps we decided to take with John. I'll give you the scoop on that in an upcoming chapter.

There was another breakthrough that came a few years later, when John's struggles over the existence of God were settled. Through those years, he would call from college to talk about his questions, and when he was home we would spend hours talking things through. But we could not make him believe. We did not try. That was not our job. God has to open the eyes of every man who comes to him. He had to open my eyes. It was up to him to open John's eyes.

The time finally came when John made the decision to believe, and when he did, there was major change. It was obvious that he had been regenerated by the Spirit of God. He began doing things he had never desired to do before—reading books, studying Scripture, praying. And that's when the Lord began to favor him with good friends and with a realization of his own calling in life.

The following summer, John decided to be a camp counselor at a Christian camp a few hours away. He wanted to help boys who were struggling as he had struggled. One weekend he came home unexpectedly. When he walked in the door, he sat down in the red chair where a few years earlier he had revealed his troubled world.

"Mom and Dad," he said, "I had to come home. I just had to come home to tell you something in person. The only way I can explain it is that once I was blind, and now I see."

There was a light in his eyes that only comes from knowing God.

I don't mind admitting it to you. Many tears had fallen around that chair. But those were the sweetest.

That's grace. That's the goodness of God.

I didn't deserve such goodness.

Had I not realized it was time to go back to square one with John and draw some lines, I might well have lost him. Had I not seen my son's great need for me at that time, I could have become an Eli or a Samuel.

And that's a sobering thought.

HOW A MAN CAN LOSE HIS SONS

So who is Eli? Before Israel had kings, they had priests. All of the other nations were led by kings, but it was God's plan that the covenant nation be led by the prophet and the priests. The priests would in turn teach and mentor their sons so that their sons could then lead the nation in the next generation.

Eli was a priest over Israel. The key to understanding Eli is actually Samuel. When Samuel was a young boy, his mother took him to the house of the Lord where he lived with Eli. Eli would serve as a mentor to Samuel. Samuel would be the last judge of Israel and a mighty prophet of the Lord. Now here's an important link. It would be Samuel whom the Lord would send to anoint Saul as the first king of Israel. And when the Lord rejected Saul, he sent Samuel to anoint David.

You can see what a key figure Samuel is to the history of Israel by the fact that two books in the Old Testament carry his name—1 and 2 Samuel.

Eli was to be the mentor to this young man who would one day have such a key role in the nation. But there was a major problem in Eli's life. His sons were priests, but they weren't qualified to be priests because they did not know the Lord:

> **Now the sons of Eli were worthless men; they did not know the Lord.... Thus the sin of the young men was very great before the Lord, for the men despised the offering of the Lord.** (1 SAMUEL 2:12, 17)

When people would bring the meat sacrifices for the priests to offer before the Lord, Eli's sons would take the portion that was for the Lord and keep it for themselves. That may not sound like a big deal, but it was the equivalent of a pastor letting his sons pilfer through the Sunday morning offering. And in the Old Testament, this was deadly serious. But the sins of Eli's sons didn't stop there:

**Now Eli was very old; and he heard all that his sons
were doing to all Israel, and how they lay with the women
who served at the doorway of the tent of the meeting.**
(1 SAMUEL 2:22)

Not only were his sons stealing the sacrifices but also they were
having sex with the women who served at the tabernacle. *Eli knew
about their sin but he did nothing about it.* Eli was a spiritual leader but he
did not give attention to his sons. He did not mentor them and he did
not teach them to love, honor, and revere the Lord.

So the Lord sent a man of God to Eli with this message:

**Why do you kick at My sacrifice and at My offering
which I have commanded in My dwelling, and honor your
sons above Me...?"** (1 SAMUEL 2:29)

Eli was so busy doing the work of ministry that he never did the
real work of ministry in his own home with his own boys. He allowed
them to break the laws of God and he refused to discipline them. And
by doing that, Eli was honoring his sons over the Lord. Because he refused to discipline his sons, God was going to discipline his sons—by
death (1 Samuel 2:34).

**"But now the Lord declares, "...for those who honor
Me I will honor, and those who despise Me will be lightly
esteemed."** (1 SAMUEL 2:30)

Eli was held responsible for the unbelief of his sons in the sense that he had refused to discipline them. Instead of fathering his sons as God had commanded, he had let them slide and get away with all kinds of things. So his boys got worse and worse because he never stepped in and took charge of them. Eli was leading in the tabernacle, but his home was out of control.

In 1 Samuel 3:12–13, the Lord speaks to young Samuel and gives him this message:

> **"In that day I will carry out against Eli all that I have spoken concerning his house, from beginning to end.**
> **For I have told him that I am about to judge his house forever for the iniquity which he knew, because his sons brought a curse on themselves and he did not rebuke them."**

It was Pearl Buck who so sagely wrote, "Every mistake has a half-way moment, a split second when it can be recalled and perhaps remedied." Eli had crossed the line. God had given him numerous opportunities to right his wrongs. But he wouldn't do it. What was needed here was a rapid response to the sin of his sons. But Eli kept coming through with no response. And that is the classic symptom of a passive father.

Passive fathers don't do what needs to be done. They sit back and do nothing. They may be aggressive in other areas of their lives. They may be highly motivated in their careers and fitness routines. But when it comes to stepping in and giving their sons the firm hand of discipline, they simply shrivel up and go passive. When a man does that, he has failed in his most important responsibility. If you have done that, it's time to get off the dime and get to work with your son.

The blind jazz pianist George Shearing loved to tell a true story on himself. He was standing at a busy intersection during rush hour, and was waiting for someone to help him cross the street. Another blind man tapped Shearing on the shoulder and asked if he would help him get across.

"What could I do?" said Shearing. "I took him across and it was the greatest thrill of my life." [5]

You've got to hand it to Shearing. He wasn't passive. That must have been quite a sight to see one blind man leading another across the intersection. It's too bad that Eli didn't have the courage to move out that Shearing did.

The tragedy is that none of this needed to happen. But Eli wouldn't step up to the plate and do the most important work. He wouldn't remedy his mistakes with his sons. He refused to do it time and time again. He thought that his most important work was in the tabernacle. God said his most important work was in his home. But he loved the ministry more than he loved the hard work with his sons. He wouldn't deny himself and take up his cross. So sadly, it came to this.

In his book on the life of Samuel, Henry Blackaby puts it plainly and clearly: "You cannot neglect your family while you minister." James Dobson Sr. understood this when he left his evangelistic ministry and came home. Apparently, Eli didn't get it. Or wouldn't get it. His sons were in sin but he was just as much in sin for refusing to discipline them. His neglect cost him not only his life, but the lives of his sons (1 Samuel 2:29–34; 4:10–18).

A Lesson Unlearned

You would think that this would have been a staggering lesson to young Samuel. But it wasn't. If we jump to 1 Samuel 8 we get the rest of the story:

> **And it came about when Samuel was old that he appointed his sons judges over Israel. . . . His sons, however, did not walk in his ways, but turned aside after dishonest gain and took bribes and perverted justice. (v. 1, 3)**

Now we're looking at Samuel's evil sons! Watch carefully what comes in the very next verses:

> **Then all the elders of Israel gathered together and came to Samuel at Ramah, and they said to him, "Behold, you have grown old, and your sons do not walk in your ways. Now appoint a king for us to judge us like all the nations.**

This is a huge moment in the history of Israel.

The reason that the people wanted a king to lead them instead of the sons of Samuel was that he had failed in his role as a father and mentor to his sons. If he had done the job at home, they would not have been looking for a king.

Blackaby observes this tragic situation with great insight:

Is it possible to be in a position of significant spiritual leadership and lose your family? Both Eli and Samuel lost their families while being the most significant spokesmen for God in their day.

Your ministry to God's people is not a substitute for your ministering before God and your family. God is looking for a godly seed. What you do in your family may determine whether God fulfills a much larger purpose than He ever had with you alone.[6]

If Eli and Samuel had done their primary jobs—the most important job of a father and a leader—there never would have been the need for a king in Israel. Their sons would have provided the leadership that the nation so desperately needed.

When these two men lost their sons, they lost a whole lot more.

Neither one of them gave their sons the attention they deserved. For most of his life, David didn't either. He blew it big time. But he decided to try and get it right with Solomon.

Proverbs 19:18 says, "Discipline your son while there is hope."

Eli didn't do that and neither did Samuel. David finally stepped up and did it. And I had to do it. When John was in trouble, it was Proverbs 19:18 that echoed in my mind on a daily, if not hourly, basis.

RECOVERING FROM OUR MISTAKES

Fathers will make mistakes. You and I will not be the exception. "All have sinned and fall short of the glory of God" (Romans 3:23). We don't want to make mistakes, and we do our best to avoid them. But the real test of a man is when he realizes at some point that he has fallen short. It was Cardinal de Retz who observed, "The man who can own up to his error is greater than he who merely knows how to avoid making it."

What would have happened if Eli had been willing to own up to his poor fathering? What if he had heeded the warnings of God and disciplined his boys? He was Samuel's primary mentor. If he had done what needed to be done, he would have been an example for Samuel to follow.

Let's take this a step further. What if Samuel had learned from Eli's mistakes? How about your family? Was your father teachable? Did he listen to the Lord and willingly do the right thing when it needed to be done? If he didn't, then you can. You can be the one to start the ball rolling in your family tribe. Why not learn from your dad's mistakes instead of repeating them?

Here is C. H. Spurgeon's version of Proverbs 22:6: "Train up a child in the way in which you now know you should have gone."

The difference between a good dad and a bad one is not perfection. The difference is the ability to recognize your mistakes and to learn from them. It was Jonathan Swift who observed that "a man should never be ashamed to own he has been in the wrong, which is but saying, in other words, that he is wiser today than he was yesterday."

Let's go one step further. My son needs to know *how* to recover from his bad choices and mistakes. It's one of the most important things he could possibly learn. But if my son never sees how I recover from mistakes, where will he learn it?

How quick are you to respond to the Spirit of God when he convicts you of a specific sin?

Eli and Samuel were slow. The Lord had spoken to each of them time and time again about their sons, but they did not respond. They knew what the Lord wanted them to do, but for some reason they put it off and told themselves there was plenty of time.

When you screw up before the Lord, you can't put your sin on hold. You have to move on it. Eli and Samuel had work to do with their sons, yet they had no sense of urgency.

Thomas Watson described the process well when he wrote, "By delay of repentance, sin strengthens, and the heart hardens. The longer ice freezes, the harder it is to be broken."

Eli and Samuel let sin linger and their own hearts became hard. And as they lingered, the sin in the hearts of their sons got stronger. It was a double-edged sword that was killing both them and their sons.

Perhaps their own unwillingness to deal with sin swiftly encouraged the same behavior in the hearts of their sons. Extract the *perhaps* from the previous sentence. Fathers who are slow to deal with sin will encourage that same slow response in the lives of their sons.

RAPID RESPONSE

Are you going to screw up? Yes. Am I going to screw up? Absolutely. So what do we do when we screw up and sin? You must deal with it swiftly. And when you deal with it swiftly, before sin strengthens and your heart hardens, then your son will learn from your example.

Your son doesn't need a dad who does it right every time. He just needs to see a dad who is in there giving it the best shot he has. And when he has blown it, he admits it—without excuses or casting of blame—and then steps up to make the necessary changes in his life. And he does it rapidly. You've heard of "rapid response teams"? That's what God wants from the men who are on his team. When He convicts you of sin—and He will do it the moment sin occurs—He then expects a rapid response of repentance.

Eli and Samuel were to discipline their sons while there was hope. They took their sweet time about it and then discovered they had waited too long. Thomas Fuller was right: "You cannot repent too soon, because you do not know how soon it may be too late."

Have you got hope to do what you need to do?

Yes.

Do you have time to wait on it?

You know the answer to that one.

You can't recover from a mistake if you don't move on the mistake.

You can't recover from sin unless you move on sin.

PRODIGALS

It is possible to raise a son right and for him to rebel. It is possible not to be an Eli and still watch your son run away from you and the Lord. Sons who are raised in the best of homes can choose to sin and pursue wrong friends and wrong choices. Fathers can model faith but they cannot instill it in the hearts of their children. Only the Holy Spirit can do that.

I have two friends whom I respect greatly. They both have walked with the Lord for over thirty years. In my estimation, they are model husbands and fathers. In both of their cases, all of their adult children are walking with the Lord—except one. Each of these men has a prodigal son.

I will tell you this. These men have followed biblical principles in leading their families. These men are not Elis. They are not even close. They have not honored their sons above the Lord. They love their sons, but they have corrected them when it was necessary and appropriate.

They are not Elis, yet they both have a son who is away from the Lord. Let me correct that. Up until last month they both had an adult son away from the Lord. But through an utterly remarkable chain of providential events, God has brought one son to love and follow Christ. I can tell you that my friend and his wife are thankful beyond words.

My other friend is still waiting and praying for God to do his work in the heart of his son. This father prays constantly for his son. He is in contact with him frequently over the telephone. This man is doing the biblical work of fathering to the best of his ability. He has said some hard things that his son didn't want to hear. He has not been passive. This man is doing all he can do before the Lord.

But he can't do the work of the Holy Spirit. He cannot change his son's heart. Perhaps you have a son or daughter in the same situation. So what do you do? You do your fathering work as best you can before the Lord. And then you wait on the heavenly Father to do his work. He's working even though you don't see a shred of evidence to support that. As you wait, He's working. It's in the Book right about Isaiah 64:4: "No eye has seen any God besides You, who acts on behalf of those who wait for him" (NIV).

In my worst moments I would swirl that verse around in my mind.

While you're waiting, God is working even when you can't see it.

So don't lose heart. Your son needs a new heart. And that new heart is worth the wait.

One father is worth more than a hundred schoolmasters.

—OLD ENGLISH PROVERB

CHAPTER FOUR

SWIFT BOOT

(MENTORING THROUGH DISCIPLINE, PART 1)

HE WAS PROPPED UP IN HIS LEATHER CHAIR, FEVERISHLY WORKING to finish before the cancer took his last breath.

He had won many battles in his day, but this was a battle he knew he was going to lose. He could no longer speak and the pain was close to unbearable. But he was determined not to die until he finished writing his story. He would indeed finish the book, just four days before the throat cancer finished him off.

The year was 1885, and in spite of the pain, he was still able to think clearly. He had grown up with a wonderful and kind father. His father had been prosperous in business when most men where struggling to make a living from the soil. As a result, he was sent to the best schools in his region, which was a privilege that few boys were given. He had been a pleasant sort of son. His father never raised his voice and never disciplined him. Unlike most boys of his day, he had probably been given too much.[1]

Yes, he had to work and do his chores, but there was plenty of time to ride his horse and skate on the ice when the pond was frozen. But childhood can't last forever. At seventeen he was completely at a loss about what he should do with his life. He had been to the best schools but had not done well. He was not interested in anything other than horses and had no interest in the family business. He was without purpose and direction. He had no drive, no ambition or aspiration for anything as he stood on the brink of manhood. He was content for his life to continue just as it was. He was so confused and aimless that his friends actually gave him the nickname of "useless."

His father was in a quandary. Time was running out. And then he got an idea. He knew what his son needed. He needed discipline, structure, order, and purpose. So he went to see an old friend who was now a congressman. The congressman agreed to the father's request. When the father returned home, he told his son that he had arranged an appointment for him at West Point.

His son didn't want to go to West Point. But his father put his foot down and insisted. His son fervently resisted. But his father would not be deterred. Off he went, almost kicking and screaming, to the famous military academy.

You've heard of swift boats? His father gave him the swift boot.

When he returned home for the first time, his family was shocked at the transformation. He had become a man, a confident young man. A young man with an internal sense of destiny and gyroscope of direction that had not been there before he had left home. And he had met a young lady, whom he would soon marry and love all the days of his life.

No one was calling him "useless" anymore. Now they were calling him by his real name, Ulysses.

Ulysses S. Grant would have his struggles in life as all men do. Yet, it was this "useless" young man of seventeen who would go on to win the Civil War and become president of the United States. When he was president and news of his father's death reached him, Grant's grief was devastatingly deep.[2] As Grant recounts in his autobiography, he could not be comforted. He knew how critical a role his father had played in his life. Without his father stepping in and redirecting his confused and aimless life by making him do what he didn't want to do, his life would have been very mediocre. Ulysses S. Grant knew that as he looked back over the pages of his life, he owed everything to his father.

One historian wrote, "The Civil War made Grant. Up until 1861, there was every chance that he would have been remembered by his friends as one of those pleasant, ineffectual fellows—the sort of person 'it is just too bad about,' a failure in everything except his marriage. Then came the war and he mastered every challenge."[3]

Yet we learn from his own words that in actuality it was not the Civil War that made Grant. West Point made Grant. But Grant would never have made it to West Point without his father stepping in and *making* him go to West Point. Jesse Root Grant had been too easy on his son and had given him too much. There was just a small window of opportunity left that could save his son from being useless and confused. Jesse Root Grant made the contact that got his son the appointment. "The harsh plebe summer, the rigid discipline, the spit and polish, the painstaking attention to detail"[4] made all the difference in a son who was on the brink of disaster. At the critical moment, in spite of his past lapses and shortcomings as a father, he took the tough step and did what needed to be done. In so doing, he saved his seventeen-year-old son from a wasted life.

DISCIPLINE WHILE THERE IS HOPE

Most dads can't pull a few strings and get their sons into West Point. Even if they could, the chances of a "useless" son getting into West Point these days are slim and none. And as they say in Texas, Slim just left town.

However, *every* dad can do for his son in his years growing up what Grant Sr. neglected to do. Every dad can give his son the structure and discipline that he needs in order to become a responsible man. Grant Sr. waited until it was almost too late. But you can't afford to do that. In this society, you have about eighteen years to do the job. Once he is eighteen and has the keys to his car (or someone else's), or can simply walk out the door, he is legally free under the laws of the land to do as he wishes. At that point, your opportunities for serious discipline have passed you. He is no longer under your authority.

Is your son over eighteen? Has he rejected you and the Lord? Then your work is not done. But it has significantly changed. Later in this book we are going to look at some very hopeful insights as to how you can build new bridges to his heart. But permit me to focus for a next few pages on those first crucial eighteen years. And, if your son is now a father, may this chapter grant you wisdom as to how you might be a godly grandfather to your son's son.

Solomon put it well:

> **Foolishness is bound up in the heart of a child;**
> **The rod of discipline will remove it far from him.**
> **(PROVERBS 22:15)**

ERADICATING FOOLISHNESS

God has commanded you to see to it that your son grows up to be a man of wisdom instead of a fool. Consider this.

If you let a young boy have his own way he will never go to bed.

His next decision will be to never get out of bed.

Neither of those is going to work.

To live that way is foolish.

The last thing you want in life is a foolish son.

As you may know, God granted to Solomon the gift of wisdom. And in his book of Proverbs, he had some choice things to say about foolish sons and the pain that they cause.

> **A wise son makes a father glad,**
> **But a foolish son is a grief to his mother. (PROVERBS 10:1)**

> **He who sires a fool does so to his sorrow,**
> **And the father of a fool has no joy. (PROVERBS 17:21)**

> **A foolish son is a grief to his father**
> **And bitterness to her who bore him. (PROVERBS 17:25)**

Is it possible to raise a son who isn't foolish? Of course it is. But it's going to take some focused and consistent effort. It is, however, an effort certainly worth making.

Every son—yours included—has the great potential of becoming a wise, responsible man. He just needs a father who is *very intentional* about building that wisdom into his life.

This is where King David went wrong with his older sons.

SONS, CHEVYS, AND SIN

Your son is not a blank slate of innocence upon which you may write. The culture embraces this idea, in spite of all contrary evidence. Many even in the church believe this. But they've missed it on this one—big time.

Every man starts out his life being foolish. *His natural tendency is to gravitate toward irresponsibility and self-centeredness.*

And here is the reason why. Every infant is born a sinner. The theological word for this is *depraved*. The biblical idea of "the depravity of man" is that every man is born with the natural inclination to sin, and that every part of his being is permeated by this inclination. "There is none who does good, there is not even one.... For all have sinned and fall short of the glory of God" (Romans 3:12, 23). The book of Romans teaches that all men, from Adam's sons onward, have been born sinners by nature. That is the tragic state in which we would still be if it were not for the grace of God through Jesus Christ!

The term *total depravity* doesn't mean that we are as depraved as we could be. It means that every aspect of our beings has been infected with sin.

I have a friend who borrowed his dad's brand-new Chevy when he was a senior in high school. He was going to the homecoming dance and his dad let him take the car. It was less than a week old. He was double-dating with another guy and everything was going just fine. Until his friend got drunk. They dropped off the girls and on the way back, his buddy crawled in the backseat because he was feeling so sick. Then he vomited all over the backseat.

My friend took the car to a twenty-four hour, self-service car wash and cleaned everything up. But that new car smell had been replaced by the smell of vomit. It was everywhere. He got up early in the morning and took the car to another car wash, where they steam-cleaned the seats and the carpet. When he got in the car, the smell of vomit was still present.

When he got home, his dad got in the car and started to pull out of the driveway. Then he suddenly stopped. The stench of vomit had reached his nostrils. And my friend was in deep trouble. They were never able to eradicate the smell of vomit from that car. It had totally permeated every seam and crevice of the upholstery. It was down deep in the foam under the seat. It was in the carpet and under it. That horrible stench had invaded every fiber of that interior.

That's what sin has done to us.

Every human is born not basically good but basically sinful. The smell and death of Adam's sin is in every one of us when we come out of the womb.

Depravity means that every child will act upon his inborn nature without any encouragement whatsoever. Did you have to teach your son to lie? Did you have to teach him to say no? He is a sinner by nature—which he acquired from you. It's in his DNA. You were born with that same bent, just like your father. "All of us like sheep have gone astray, each of us has turned to his own way" (Isaiah 53:6).

So what does this have to do with foolishness? The fact that he is a sinner means that *he will fight the very things that are good for him*. That's what fools do. And that's why you are there. You are there to train him to turn away from his natural foolishness and lead him toward wisdom.

Every dad knows what I'm talking about. When a child is little, he doesn't want to go to bed. He wants to eat sugar instead of meats and vegetables. He wants you to buy every toy he sees in the toy store. He'll watch TV for endless hours or play Nintendo until he can't see straight. When he can't get his way, he'll scream and kick or just whine and fuss and argue you to death, all in the hope against hope that he might get his way.

When he gets older, he'll fight with his siblings until you think you are going insane. He'll grumble about doing his chores. He'll do everything he can to postpone doing his homework. He'll talk back to you or flat-out disobey you just to see if he can get away with it. He'll beg to have the latest thing everyone else has—and he will use the age-old guilt trip to trick you into getting it for him. He will argue with you about whatever reasonable limitations you have placed in his life. Why? Because he wants to be happy and free. He doesn't understand that happiness and freedom without responsibility and maturity is destructive to his health.

In short, he will do a pretty good job of driving you nuts.

You just can't let him get away with it.

DIFFERENT PERSONALITIES, SAME PROBLEM

Linebacker, quarterback, and tackle are positions in football. Strong-willed, manipulator, and compliant are dispositions in children. That means that sons will express their sinfulness in very different ways.

Some sons will fight their parents openly and relentlessly. They'll fight you to get their way pretty much from the time they learn to say "mama" and "dada." (These are known as the "strong-willed" sons.) Other sons will try to smooth their way out of responsibility or just merely postpone it. They will use every excuse in the book, even resorting to going to mom as a buffer. They are great at using their witty, winsome personalities. (These are the "manipulators.")

A third kind of son will quietly and almost easily comply. This is the child who can slip under the radar, because you will breathe a sigh of relief and say, "Finally, a kid who gets it." But let me give you a warning—after years of experience with watching compliant children mature into adulthood in good families I've known well for years. The compliant child is the one you must hone in on very closely. You have to work extra hard at getting to know him. And if in his compliance he begins to exhibit an unmasculine passivity, or unhealthy noncommunication and silence, this is the son you especially want to watch. These sons risk becoming part of the new *passive-nonaggressive* Seinfelds of our times. Why? Because these sons want to please, and they hate confrontation. So they find it hard to express their real and true feelings. As a result, they will simply go underground to avoid it.

Submarines run silent and they run deep. That's how compliant sons run. They submerge what's really going on inside of them. Do you have a son like that? Underneath this kind of compliant passiveness can be a harboring of feelings (legitimate or illegitimate) of hurt and anger. And the longer it smolders, the harder this son will be to reach.

Could these things be resolved through healthy communication? Sure they can. But if he isn't one to naturally expose his true feelings, and if for some reason he doubts that he will really be understood or heard, the underground anger and hurt will go on doing their quiet destructive work. He may be compliant now and easy now. But that hidden and unresolved anger will eventually turn him into an angry, rebellious young man.

Which is your son? Maybe you have one of each. If he is strong-willed, it could mean World War III. This is not a war of bombs and machine guns. It is a *war of the wills*. And this, gentlemen, is a war you absolutely must win. He's got to know that the world does not revolve around him. He cannot win. He cannot control your home. He cannot call the shots. Period. But when you wage this war, you must do it with calm, loving, but firm and resolute authority. Don't draw boundaries one day and then waver on the next. In war, there has to be rules. And your son must know that you mean what you say. By the way, the earlier in his life that you begin—*age one* is not too young—the better, and the more certain you can be of an *early* victory.

If, on the other hand, your son is the manipulator, you will need to see through his manipulation and let him know you see through it. Just because he delights you and knows how to make you laugh doesn't stop him from foolishness. In fact, some of the greatest fools are some of the funniest, most amiable people on earth. Obedience is not an option to be joked about, excused, or bargained over. Obedience is literally a matter of life and death.

What I am saying is that *to be an effective disciplinarian, you've got to know your son.* You've got to know what makes him tick. And not tick. It's going to take some time to get to know him. Quite a bit of time. Just that piece of information may tick you off. But it's better to be ticked off up front than to miss the tick in your son's heart.

WHAT EVERY SON WANTS: DISCIPLINE AND UNDERSTANDING

Every son *wants to be disciplined.* He needs it. He may not let on at first, but the happiest son on earth is the son who has been appropriately disciplined. Biblical discipline actually relieves a son. It lets him know that his father really loves him. It's as if the air has been cleared, life has been put back in order as God intended it to be, and everyone can breathe and enjoy life as it should be enjoyed.

But every son also *wants to be understood* by his dad. I cannot emphasize this enough. David didn't understand Absalom. Now Absalom had some serious problems in his own life. But he was legitimately enraged that his sister had been raped. If that were your sister, wouldn't you feel the same way?

David didn't seem to fully get it. He didn't understand Absalom's righteous anger regarding the heinous rape of his sister. David didn't listen to Absalom's repeated appeals to his father for justice on her behalf. Then when his son in desperation brutally took matters into his own hands, David simply looked at the hard-core facts at hand and shut Absalom out of his life—forever. So much for building bridges. So much for redemption in any form. David took the easy way out. He ignored his son. He loved him, but he ignored him. And it turned out to be disastrous.

It was over Absalom that David experienced his greatest grief. "O, my son, Absalom, my son, Absalom, my son, my son!" He wept uncontrollably once he had learned of his untimely death (2 Samuel 18:33). Absalom was the son who had nearly cost him his kingdom. Yet Absalom had been the son who had grabbed the heart of David more than any of his other boys. Alexander Whyte captures well the emotions that must have been in David's heart:

> "The pang of the cry, innermost agony of the cry, the poisoned
> point of the dagger in that cry is remorse. I have slain my son! I have
> murdered my son with my own hands! I neglected my son Absalom
> from a child. With my own lusts I have laid his very worst tempta-
> tion right in his way. It would have been better if he had never been

born. If he rebelled, who should blame him? I, David, drove Absalom to rebellion.'"[5]

If a dad disciplines without ever taking the time to get to know his son and truly understand him, his discipline can actually turn out to be counterproductive. And that is exactly what happened to David. That's why he had such great remorse over Absalom.

GETTING TO KNOW WHAT MAKES HIM TICK

The story is told of a northerly midwestern village on the shores of the Great Lakes before refrigeration was invented. Every winter the community of men would come together to cut up huge blocks of ice from the frigid lakes and haul them into an icehouse. Once enclosed there, the ice would stay frozen throughout the upcoming summer. It was a laborious, exhausting job, and all the young boys would come alongside to help. One day one of the workers realized that he had lost his watch. In those days watches were valuable and not easily replaced. Everyone to a man ceased his work and began the search. But it was nowhere to be found. By late afternoon all had given up hope of ever finding the watch—except for one small boy. An idea had hatched in his mind. And so, once everyone had gone home and no one was looking, he snuck into the icehouse. He lay there on the frigid floor, still as a mouse. All was silent. For some time, he heard only the howling of the wind and the occasional brushing of branches against the walls of the icehouse. Then he heard it. "Tick-tock. Tick-tock. Tick-tock." He jumped up and began digging at the very point of the sound. And there it was. The watch had fallen in between some chunks of ice and hay, just waiting to be discovered. It took a little boy to figure out that the best way to find a watch was to lie still and listen for it!

Once again, we're back to the innermost beat of your son's life. How does a dad hear the "tick-tock" of his son's heart? It certainly isn't going to happen just running around on a sports field, or racing through a "to do" list at breakneck speed with his son, or pushing through twenty pages of math problems. You might glean a little knowledge about him, but you probably won't get very far inside his heart.

You've got to have some down time to hear the ticking of his heart.

So some guys hunt. Take your son with you.

Some guys go fishing. Take your boy with you, and you'll have plenty of time to hear the tick-tock.

I know one guy who takes a motorcycle trip each summer with his teenage son. They plan a ten-day trip and cover a lot of highway. And they've got plenty of time to talk in the evenings.

I think you get the idea.

You've got to purposefully design a time of quiet where you can hear the inside of your son's heart. And one more thing. The older he gets, the more important these times will be. Why? Because he's getting closer to manhood every day and you've only got so much time left to be with him.

It's on getaways like this that he will begin to open up his heart and let you know what's going on inside. It's just the two of you without any interruptions. No friends, no video games, no school, no phone calls. Good things come out of deals like that.

The better you know him, the better you will be as a father.

The better you know him, the more effective will be your discipline. The more time he has with you and the better his relationship with you, the less he will resent your discipline. Josh McDowell has said it for years:

"Rules without relationship equals rebellion."

And that brings me to a final point in this chapter on discipline. Last night Josh asked me if I was going to address fathers who are overbearing. I told him that I was. I'm going to deal with it in a later chapter in detail, but for now, here's the real short version.

God has called you to be his father, not a jerk.

He's going to have enough jerks in his life that are always on his case and nitpicking everything he does. Make sure that's not you.

When fathers get overly harsh in their discipline and in the atmosphere that they set in the home, sons get angry. And they are right to be angry. When fathers are jerks they are in absolute disobedience to the Word of God:

> **Fathers, do not provoke your children to anger,**
> **but bring them up in the discipline…of the Lord.**
> **(EPHESIANS 6:4)**

Do children get angry when they are disciplined? You bet they do. That's part of being a kid. But when discipline is correct and even, they know in their hearts it is the right thing. They may still be angry, but they know that they received what they deserved.

That's different than the anger that comes from discipline that is overly harsh and doesn't fit the offense.

In Ephesians 6:4, *Paul is talking about an authoritarian, controlling, unkind, overly-severe discipline which produces a long-term anger, the kind of anger that leads to alienation between father and son*—and eventual rebellion against God. Biblical discipline has an entirely different look from unbiblical discipline. One is characterized by loving but resolute firmness. The other is characterized by harsh anger. One epitomizes *discipline in the father*. The other epitomizes *a lack of discipline in the father*.

And believe me, sons instinctively know the difference.

> **Fathers, do not exasperate your children, so that they will not lose heart.** (COLOSSIANS 3:21)

A son knows when his father is disciplining out of firmness and godly authority. And he knows when he isn't. A harsh and authoritarian father can have a devastating impact on his family. In a later chapter, we will look at the harshness that crept into Solomon's heart and the impact it had not only on his son, but also on the entire nation.

So how much do you discipline? How do you know where the line is between justice and harshness? In my mind, that's a cooking question.

JULIA CHILD CAN'T DISCIPLINE YOUR CHILD

Julia Child was one of the greatest cooks in the world. I'm not. As a matter of fact, I don't cook at all. But I was reading an article somewhere the other day about a guy who was a great chef.[6] It mentioned in the article that one of his hobbies was collecting antique cookbooks. Quite frankly, that sounds pretty dull to me. But the more I read, the more I discovered why this chef collected antique cookbooks. It turns out that old cookbooks would give the ingredients of a recipe but never the measurements. That was something the cook had to figure out. Can you imagine trying to make mouth-watering lasagna by knowing the ingredients but not the measurements? So does it take a teaspoon of oregano or half a quart? Who could imagine a cookbook with ingredients but no measurements?

God does the same thing in the Scriptures. When God gives you a family, he gives you a cookbook with all the ingredients and none of the measurements. Figuring out the right measurements is what separates the men from the boys. Getting the measurements right is what separates a poor father from a good father. Mixing the right amount of love and discipline for each child is an awe-inspiring challenge. Every kid needs discipline—but some need more than others. Discipline is the ingredient—but how much do you measure out? Therein lies the challenge.

> **Work out your salvation with fear and trembling,**
> **for it is God who is at work in you, both to will and to work**
> **for His good pleasure. (PHILIPPIANS 2:12–13)**

You desperately need the Lord to give you the wisdom to dispense just the right amount of discipline. If it's too much, you'll be harsh. If it's too little, you'll be soft and ineffective. That's why you need the Lord. But if you seek him, he'll dish out his wisdom to you in just the right amounts. And then your discipline will not only be measured . . . it will be effective. That's how you discipline with confidence.

MURDERING MURDER

Jonathan Edwards is regarded by many scholars as the greatest thinker that America ever produced. This godly pastor and former president of Princeton University was a prolific preacher, scholar, philosopher, and scientist. He was born in 1703 and died in 1758 of a smallpox inoculation. He had a great love for Jesus Christ and his Word. He and his wife, Sarah, had eleven children, and they were considered a model family. In fact, a study has been done of the over 1400 descendants that followed Edwards. It is a remarkable legacy of responsible and disciplined individuals who contributed to society.

What is not as commonly known is the story of Jonathan Edwards' grandmother. In a day when divorce and adultery were unheard of, she was found by her husband to be pregnant with another man's child just shortly after they were married. For the rest of her life, she lived a life of open sexual immorality. Elizabeth Tuthill Edwards pursued a life of sexual perversity that brought shame and anguish upon her family. She was a woman of violence and rage who threatened to cut the throat of her husband while he slept. [7] How would you like to have a grandmother like that?

The threat to murder her husband was no idle threat. Elizabeth's sister also displayed rage and violence to such a degree that she murdered her own child. How would you like to have a great-aunt like that?

Elizabeth also had a brother who, in a fit of rage, killed one of his sisters with an ax. How would you like to have an uncle like that?

Jonathan Edwards came from a family that acquainted him first-hand with the reality of sin. Edwards wanted to take his own family a different direction. He was concerned about the strain of violence, murder, anger, and immorality that ran through his family line.

So he became intentionally involved in the lives of his children. He made sure he spent at least one hour a day in purposeful interaction with at least one of his children. Second, he realized that sin was real and foolishness was bound up in the heart of child. So he disciplined his children.

But as he disciplined, he made sure that he was connected.

Perhaps it was due to the fact that his mentoring was so purposeful that murder was never again seen in the direct descendants of Edwards, although it occurred twice in a previous generation.

Edwards didn't sit on his heels like Eli and hope for the best.

Jonathan Edwards got with the program.

He got involved and he got connected. And it made a huge difference in the generations that followed.

That's a program worth signing up for.

It is common sense to put the seal

to the wax while it is still soft.

—ARTHUR JACKSON

FREEDOM MAN

(MENTORING THROUGH DISCIPLINE, PART 2)

THERE ARE THREE ISSUES THAT ALL GO TOGETHER.

Gun control, sword control, and son control.

In the Old Testament when Saul became the first king of Israel, they didn't have gun control. That's because they didn't have guns. But they did have sword control and spear control. To be more precise, they had blacksmith control. And it was imposed upon them by their enemies, the Philistines. First Samuel 13:19–23 says:

> Now no blacksmith could be found in all the land of Israel, for the Philistines said, "Otherwise the Hebrews will make swords or spears." So all Israel went down to the Philistines, each to sharpen his plowshare, his mattock, his axe, and his hoe. The charge was two-thirds of a shekel for the plowshares, the mattocks, the forks, and the axes, and to fix the hoes. So it came about on the day

of the battle that neither sword nor spear was found in the hands of any of the people who were with Saul and Jonathan, but they were found with Saul and his son Jonathan.

Fidel Castro took power in 1959 by leading a revolt against the dictator, Fulgencio Batista. Castro instituted gun control and registration. Then he immediately confiscated every gun and rifle on the island. And as a result, for nearly fifty years the citizens of Cuba have had no ability to fight against their wicked tyrant. The citizens of Cuba lost their freedom.[1]

The Philistines did the same thing to Israel. They got rid of all the blacksmiths and when they did that, they got rid of any new swords or spears. And they took it one step further. If you needed a tool sharpened, you had to go down to Gaza and have a Philistine blacksmith do the job for you. If you dared to walk in there with a sword, they would confiscate it.

That's why none of the people who went to battle with Saul and Jonathan had any swords or spears. They had lost their freedom.

What does this have to do with disciplining sons?

Nothing. I just wanted to make a point about gun control.

Actually, I'm just kidding. There is a correlation and here it is.

Fathers are to sons what blacksmiths are to swords.

It is the job of the blacksmith not only to make a sword but also to maintain its edge of sharpness.

It is the job of the father to keep his son sharp and save him from the dullness of foolishness. He gives his son that sharp edge through discipline.

Fathers are to sons what blacksmiths are to swords.

FROM SELF-CENTEREDNESS TO SELF-DISCIPLINE

The most important thing you will ever do for your son is to discipline him. You do it because you love him and you don't want him to grow up to be a foolish man. Discipline is *your* primary job description.

The father's job is to move his son *from self-centeredness to self-discipline*. And when that happens, that father has given his son the gift of freedom.

What is self-discipline? It is saying no to foolish behavior so that he can say yes to the destiny and purpose that God has for his life.

There are certain traits of a self-disciplined man. And these are the traits that you want to instill in your son. Your goal is that he will eventually become his own disciplinarian—a spiritual self-starter:

- *A self-disciplined son learns to control his emotions and drives. In other words, he can put a cap on his anger and exercise control in his sex life.*
- *A self-disciplined son respects authority, even when he doesn't agree with it.*
- *A self-disciplined son grasps the value of future reward over immediate gratification.*
- *A self-disciplined son has learned to see outside his own little world of his own needs. In fact, he sees it as his honor and duty to sacrifice to meet the needs of those he loves.*
- *A self-disciplined son is a self-starter. He doesn't need his mom to get him up every morning so that he won't be late for his senior English class.*

Now these are goals. They don't happen overnight. But when a dad faithfully, consistently works with his son—"trains him," as the Bible calls it—over the years of his son's development into manhood, he will begin to see the fruit.

> **All discipline for the moment seems not to be joyful, but sorrowful; yet to those who have been trained by it, afterwards it yields** *the peaceful fruit of righteousness.* **(HEBREWS 12:11, italics mine)**

There is no greater joy than to see the fruit of discipline in your son's life. There's no greater happiness than when your son becomes *his own disciplinarian.*

And that's when your son will take off like a self-propelling rocket.

The story is told of the real estate agent that was out looking at ranches one afternoon. As he was driving down the country highway he noticed a chicken running alongside his car. He couldn't believe his eyes because he was going about 55 mph. He sped up and the chicken stayed with him. As he looked closer, it appeared that the chicken had three legs. Suddenly, the chicken hit the afterburners and pulled way ahead of him, only slowing to make a left turn on a gravel road.

The agent decided to follow the chicken. Before long, he came to a farm and saw a farmer out by the barn.

"Sir, did you happen to see a three-legged chicken go by here?"

"I sure did. In fact, she's one of mine. I breed 'em. People always ask me why, and the answer is real simple. When we have chicken dinner, I love the drumstick, my wife wants a drumstick, and my son wants a drumstick. We were always coming up short until I starting breeding these chickens."

"Well, how do they taste?" asked the agent.

"I don't rightly know," said the farmer. "I've never been able to catch one."

You're raising your son to become self-disciplined. And when that happens, he'll take off like one of those chickens. When a chicken gets three legs, that's freedom. When a son becomes self-disciplined, he's free for the first time in his life. But there's a very important step before he will get to that point.

RESPONSIBILITY AND PRIVILEGE

Here's the formula: Responsibility = Privilege

Responsibility leads to privileges and new freedoms. Not the other way around. Too many of us fathers have given our sons way too much too soon. I did that with John when he was in high school. And when we do this, our sons fail to learn a valuable lesson.

- *Privilege is not an inborn, inherited right.*
- *Privilege is the result of responsible character.*

Let's say that your son never learns to obey authority, thinks the world revolves around him, and has never been disciplined when he lies or acts disrespectfully. Jeremiah Burroughs observed that "there is little hope of children who are educated in wickedness. If the dye has been in the wool, it's hard to get it out of the cloth."

Discipline must begin early. If that kind of foolishness is not disciplined, there is going to be some grief in that family before it's all over with. That kid could very easily wind up in jail if those behaviors are not dealt with early. You may think that is an extreme statement. But just ask the Enron executives who are doing time if there isn't some truth in it.

How many privileges will your son have in jail?

How many privileges will your son enjoy in solitary confinement?

You may be saying, "My son isn't even in kindergarten. What could this possibly have to do with me?" Let me relate an incident that occurred when our John was only three.

SNEAK PREVIEW

When John had just turned three years old, he had an experience he has never forgotten. Mary was giving his six-week-old baby brother a bath in the kitchen sink when the doorbell rang. We had taught John that if you are ever in real trouble and there is nobody to help you, you can dial 911. And he had learned how to do that. "Don't ever do this unless you are really in trouble," we had said. So while Mary was busy in the kitchen, he had snuck into the bedroom, picked up the phone, and pushed 911 with his stubby little fingers. No sooner had the operator answered, he hung up. A few minutes later, a police officer showed up at the front door. Mary greeted him with a sopping baby in her arms and John holding on to her skirts.

"Hello, ma'am. We just received a 911 emergency call from this address. Is anything wrong?"

Mary was stunned. "Are you sure you have the right address?"

"Yes, ma'am. Is this…?" and he gave our home phone number.

"Why, yes it is. Well, Officer, I'm so sorry for this mistake! I can assure you that we are fine. I can't imagine who might have placed that call to you."

The officer looked down at John. A notable gleam appeared in his eyes.

"Well, ma'am," he said, "could it have possibly been your little boy who placed the call?"

John went ashen.

"John, did you dial 911?" she asked.

"No, I didn't."

"Are you sure? It's okay if you did. We just need to know," she said, leaning down and looking into his face.

"I'm sure. I didn't do it." He sounded quite convincing.

The officer, who was the wiser, looked in John's direction and very calmly explained. "Well, as you know, when somebody calls and it turns out to be a false alarm, then we can't do our real job. While we're driving over to your house, somebody else who is really in serious trouble might call. But if we're here, we can't be over there helping the people who are really in trouble. You know what I mean."

"I certainly do," Mary answered knowingly.

John blushed with shame.

"I am so very sorry that we took you away from your important work. And I can assure you that it won't happen again," she said.

"Thank you, ma'am. I'm sure that it won't." He tipped his hat at John and smiled as he walked back to his patrol car.

Mary walked with John into his bedroom and sat down for a talk. He continued to insist that he had not done it. She gently suggested the alternatives. "Well, John, I didn't do it," she said. "Maybe Josh did it," he said. He was actually suggesting that his six-week-old brother had accidentally done it. "Or maybe the officer really did make a mistake." John wasn't ready to crack. So Mary decided to leave it to me.

When I arrived home, I took John aside. I made it very clear that he couldn't cover up his sin anymore. I gently told him that his lies were far worse than the thing that he had done. Eventually he admitted the truth. Yes, he had done it. He had been curious. He had wondered if it really would work. And then when it did work, the officer had scared him so much that he had been afraid to tell the truth. Once he had lied, although he didn't say this in so many words, it was his honor that was now at stake. Honor is very important to a man, even when he is three.

"Well, John," I said, "I'm very glad you have told the truth. It's always harder to tell the truth than to tell a lie. It takes a man to tell the truth. You have done the right and the honorable thing here. You have confessed your sin. Would you like to ask God to forgive you?" He was eager to do it. So right then and there we prayed, and John told the Lord that he was truly sorry and asked for his forgiveness. It was as if a great load had been lifted from his shoulders.

"Now, John," I said, "there's one more thing that we need to do. You need to apologize to the policeman. Since you lied to him, it would be only right for you to apologize to him too." John's eyes got as big as silver dollars. "Don't worry; I'll be right there with you. And you will be surprised at how nice a man he is. He will respect you for coming and apologizing to him." This had turned into a much bigger deal than John had ever imagined.

FIELD TRIP

We headed down to the station to find the policeman. The building was a normal-sized small-town station, but it looked enormous to John. It was a very nice, brand-new facility, with officers coming and going, and three holding cells in the back. "Excuse me," I said to the officer at the front desk. "We are looking for officer (so and so)." "Oh," he said, "he's off duty right now." John was in luck. "Well," I said, and went on to explain why we were there. The officer looked down at the terrified little tyke by my side and said, "Young man, I'll be sure to pass on your message to him."

Then I got an idea. Those holding cells were empty and quite frankly, looked like they have never been used.

"Sir, would it be all right for us to look at the jail cells?"

The officer immediately picked up on my intent.

"Of course," he said as he gave me a knowing nod.

John had never seen a jail. Most three-year-olds haven't. But that's a good time for a field trip. We walked back to the group of cells. John was utterly surprised and intrigued.

"Dad," he said, "those guys have to go to the bathroom right out in front of everybody! And there are not any sheets on their bed, or any blankets. They don't even have Kleenex!" Kleenex was a big deal to John at this stage of life. He stood mesmerized for a while. Then he asked thoughtfully, "Dad, what do they do all day in there?" He didn't see any toys, or cards, or even books. It was an eye-opener for a three-year-old. I said, "Well, John, this is what happens to guys who never learn how to tell the truth. They just keep lying, and lying, and they get into more and more trouble, and before you know it, they end up in jail. This is the sad thing that happens to people who live their whole lives telling lies."

We talked about the jail all the way home. When we got home, John told his mom and his older sister all about the jail. He told his friends about the jail. In other words, the impact was pretty profound. And whenever he talked about the jail, he mentioned the fact that people who tell lies are the ones that wind up in jail. I don't think John was ever able to eradicate that lesson from his heart. When it came down to it, it was actually his ability to be truthful later in life that saved him.

What happens to a kid who never learns that with responsibility comes privilege? Sometimes he ends up in jail. Sometimes he learns it in solitary.

How many privileges and freedoms did Samson have when the Philistines blinded and imprisoned him? If you go back and read the story of Samson in Judges 13–16, you will read of a gifted, amazing young man who remained imprisoned until the end of his life. He squandered what had been given to him. And a large part of that was the result of his father's jello-ish backbone and failure to lead him to self-discipline when it came to foreign women.

Somewhere along the line, sons must be taught the relationship between responsibility and reward, between obedience and freedom. The tendency in America for the average father is to give his son way too much freedom and rewards for far too little responsibility. *The way that it should work is that if a son shows a willingness to shoulder responsibility, he will then be given more privileges and freedoms.*

Sometimes a dad wakes up late in the game to the reality of these things. And when that happens, extreme measures are in order.

EXTREME MEASURES

I have a friend named Clarke Bynum who was on an international flight to Africa one year before the destruction of September 11, 2001 (known now simply as "9-11"). No one had yet conceived of terrorists using passenger planes as suicide missles of destruction. He and his buddy Gifford Shaw had been bumped up to Business Class. Clarke was in the aisle seat and Gifford was next to the window. Because security was not a concern, the pilots actually had the cockpit door open. Suddenly, a screaming man ran down the aisle, attacked the pilots, and grabbed the controls in an attempt to crash the plane.

What would you do in that situation? People were frozen in shock as the man fought the pilots for control of the 747. Clarke, who had not been in a fight since elementary school, decided it was time to get into another. So he sprinted into the cockpit and took the guy down. It took two minutes to restrain the man. In that time, the plane went into two nosedives as the man pounded on the pilots' heads and continued to try to crash the plane. Bynum's quick thinking and courage saved the plane from disaster.

In a split second, life-and-death decisions had to be made. Time was running out. So Clarke took some extreme measures. And he averted a tragedy.

You get the point.

When you see your son in a similar nosedive, you had better move to save his life.

I know one very calm and reasonable man whose teenage son simply could not get himself out of bed in the morning. He could set three alarm clocks and you could clang cymbals in his ears for that matter, but he could not seem to get up. So his father told his son that if he was not awake the next morning and dressed by seven o'clock, he was going to throw a bucket of water on his face. His son laughed inwardly at the thought ... until the next morning when he was suddenly aroused from his sleep by a bucket of ice-cold water. The next morning and every morning after, he was up and ready by 7 a.m.

Sometimes it takes extreme measures to drive the point home.

James Dobson Sr. intuitively knew this when he put his house up for sale.

Jesse Root Grant also knew that time was running out when he sent Ulysses off to West Point.

And that's why I got rid of the Jeep. I knew the clock was ticking and I was almost out of time.

THE GOODWILL JEEP

I mentioned in an earlier chapter that I would fill you in on some of the measures we took to help John in his time of trouble. If John had gangrene moving up his leg, some extreme measures would be recommended by the doctor to save his life. In this particular period of his life, John had gangrene spreading throughout his heart. And something had to be done.

We began by establishing boundaries right up front: no more drugs and no more alcohol (since they were, for one very good reason, against the law), and no more of his bad friends. With each, there were clear consequences if the conditions weren't met. John knew the seriousness of the situation. And despite some very dark times in which he felt he was fighting the devil himself, John made the huge decision to agree to the conditions.

But we also did something to encourage him to make this decision.

We live a little way out in the country, and it was about a thirty-minute drive into school. I had bought a used Jeep so that John could drive himself and his brother to school.

One Saturday morning John came outside.

John said, "Dad, did you move my Jeep?"

"No, I gave it away."

"You what?"

"I gave it away to someone who needed a vehicle."

"But that was my Jeep."

"No, it wasn't. That's my Jeep. I was just letting you drive it."

"So how am I going to get to school?"

"There's a bus you can catch."

Now John was absolutely speechless. When his speech returned, I noticed that his hearing had also improved dramatically. We had a very clear conversation about his lack of responsibility in some critical areas.

"But Rachel had a car when she was my age."

"Yes, but she earned the privilege, John, and in your heart you know that's true. I made the mistake of giving you the same privilege at the same age. I was wrong in doing that. I'm correcting that mistake. I love you too much to continue with that privilege. You have lost the privilege because you haven't been responsible. Now you can earn it back—but it's going to take some time."

"How much time?

"That's up to you. But at a minimum, we're talking months, not weeks. I want to see some consistent changes, not short-term."

About ten months later, John's driving situation improved.

He had earned it in a number of ways. He had walked away from the drugs and the alcohol and the friends. Everything had improved around the house because his attitude had changed. And when his attitude changed, he became responsible in those areas where he had been irresponsible.

A couple of years later, John applied for a job that required him to be at work at 5:30 a.m. When he showed up on time every morning for two weeks, his boss gave him a raise. They had never had anyone in that position actually show up on time two weeks straight. Imagine getting a raise for simply showing up on time. It's called being responsible. And it began for John by losing a privilege.

UNDER THE RADAR

My good friend Joe White owns Kanakuk Kamps in Missouri (www.kanakuk.org). Thousands of kids come through these wonderful Christian camps every summer. Joe deals with a lot of kids and a lot of parents who are struggling. A lot of those parents have given their children way too much privilege, and all they are getting in return are bad attitudes, disrespect, rebellion, and laziness. So he put together a plan in the form of a little chart that captures the concept we are discussing. The value of this chart is that it is a template that lays out the relationship between responsibility and freedom for an adolescent. It can obviously be adapted to fit your particular situation. But it provides a starting point. It provides structure and clarity for attitudes and behaviors.

An adapted form of the chart, called "Taking It To The Top," is shown on the next page. It outlines the responsibilities that are necessary in order to be given freedoms.

TAKE IT TO THE TOP!

FREEDOMS	FLOOR	RESPONSIBILITIES

7

FREEDOMS
1. College
2. Car
3. Spending money
4. Hours, curfews, friends, etc. all your decisions

RESPONSIBILITIES
1. *____GPA
2. Collegiate lifestyle free of alcohol, drugs, and premarital sex
3. Pursue own solid Christian growth objectives
4. Sound career pursuit
   * (Parental discretion)

6

FREEDOMS
1. Driver's license
2. Together we share the finances of your own car
3. One–two night activities per weekend *____curfew
4. *____minutes/night telephone
5. *____/week allowance
   * (Increase Level 5)

RESPONSIBILITIES
1. *____GPA
2. Leadership in one church or parachurch organization
3. Keep car clean and serviced consistently
   * (Parental discretion)

5

FREEDOMS
1. Driver's permit
2. *____/week allowance
3. One night out per weekend *____curfew
4. *____minutes/night telephone
   * (Increase Level 4)

RESPONSIBILITIES
1. *____GPA
2. Consistent pursuit of school activity
3. Clearly communicate plans with parents
4. Success with part-time job
5. Sweep and wash car once a week
   * (Parental discretion)

4

FREEDOMS
1. One night out per weekend *____curfew
2. One *____call/night
3. One TV show (approved) per day
4. $*____/week allowance
   * (Parental discretion)

RESPONSIBILITIES
1. *____GPA
2. Up and ready for school on time
3. Pleasant attitude with mom, dad, siblings
4. Daily quiet time
5. Choice of friends (male/female) with stable Christian reputation
   * (Parental discretion)

3

FREEDOMS
1. Living at home
2. We drive you to and from school
3. No money, no phones, no nights out
4. Christian music only
5. One TV show (approved) per week

RESPONSIBILITIES
1. Constant obedience to parents and rules of home
2. Consistent deportment at school
3. No unexcused absences
4. No attempts to run away
5. *____GPA at school
6. Weekly chores
7. No foul language
8. Regular church and youth group attendance
9. No drugs, alcohol, sex
   * (Parental discretion)

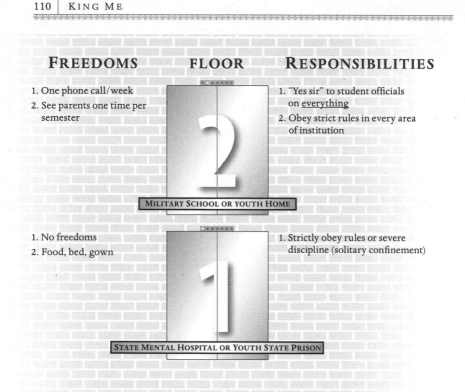

FREEDOMS	FLOOR	RESPONSIBILITIES
1. One phone call/week 2. See parents one time per semester	**2** MILITARY SCHOOL OR YOUTH HOME	1. "Yes sir" to student officials on <u>everything</u> 2. Obey strict rules in every area of institution
1. No freedoms 2. Food, bed, gown	**1** STATE MENTAL HOSPITAL OR YOUTH STATE PRISON	1. Strictly obey rules or severe discipline (solitary confinement)

In my adapted version of the chart the elevator is at the third floor, where most sons are: living at home, with a parent or bus taking the kid to school, limited TV watching, and limited freedoms. By the time the son has reached "the top" with his own car, spending money, and the privilege to set his own curfew and choose his own friends, he has proven himself by accepting more and more responsibilities.

But as the chart points out, there are two other levels to which a son may descend if he rejects responsibilities. And these two levels involve authority figures other than mom and dad. For sons who never learn to submit to authority in the home and accept responsibility, there are other institutions that have been prepared for them. One option is military school. But there are others for the hard-hearted. Juvenile detention centers and prisons are more difficult situations for the obstinate son.

And even in prison, the most basic privileges are taken away in solitary confinement.

So if a son thinks he has it tough at home, he needs to be reminded that there are other situations that are much more difficult. It's all a matter of perspective.

FEAR OF THE FATHER, FEAR OF THE FATHER

Joe's chart is one that helps a father move his son to wisdom. The principle of the chart is that privileges are rewards for responsible behavior and attitudes.

This chart will strike fear in the heart of a son because it demonstrates to him the power that is available to his father. Now follow me closely here. Because the father is the one who has the power to grant privileges and take them away—that brings about a healthy fear of a father.

I had no doubts that my dad loved me. He would do anything for me. I knew that in the deepest part of my being. He loved me so much that he would discipline me. He loved me so much that he would invoke appropriate discipline when I misbehaved. My dad was big on follow-through. That's why I feared him. I wasn't terrified of him because I knew that he loved me and would do what was best for me. And sometimes it was best that I "felt" certain consequences. That gave me a healthy fear that kept me out of a lot of trouble. It saved me from some bad situations on more than one occasion.

Your son must have a healthy fear of you and your commitment to doing what is right in his life. It's important because if your son never has a healthy fear of you, he will never have a healthy fear of God.

The fear of the Lord is the beginning of wisdom.
(**PROVERBS 9:10**)

Wisdom begins with the fear of the Lord. There are all kinds of unhealthy fears in the world. But the fear of the Lord is a healthy, life-saving fear. It's an awe and respect for the Lord and his life-giving laws. It's a belief in the absolute certainty of painful consequences when they are disobeyed.

A fool ignores the laws of God and scoffs at his warnings. A wise man fears the Lord and finds happiness in his law.

But please pay close attention here.

Fear of the heavenly Father begins with a fear of the earthly father.

If your son has no respect for you, how is he going to gain a respect for God? Whether you wish it or not, you are your son's instinctive image of God. You are the best physical representation of God to him on earth. If your son learns a healthy fear of you, then he is well on his way to fearing God.

And isn't that the goal?

A son who fears God will love his truth and discover the life God designed him to live.

Many men give up that power by giving their kids everything. When you give them everything they want when they want it, you have given up your power. And when you lose your power, you will not be feared.

When the Cubans gave up their guns, they gave up their power to defend themselves against tyrants. And for forty-five years, Castro has had no fear of the people revolting. They gave up their power a long time ago. And as a result, they have lost their freedom.

When the Jews gave up their blacksmiths to the Philistines, they lost their power to fight for their nation. And the Philistines had no fear of the Jews, because the Jews had given up their swords, their spears, and their blacksmiths. In other words, they lost their freedom.

When a father gives up his power by giving his son everything he wants, his son will not fear him in a healthy way. When there is no fear on a son's part of a father's discipline, then that son has lost his freedom.

In President Ronald Reagan's farewell address to the nation, he told a true story about a refugee and a sailor:

> It was back in the early eighties, at the height of the boat people. And the sailor was hard at work on the carrier *Midway,* which was patrolling the South China Sea. The sailor, like most American servicemen, was young, smart, and fiercely observant. The crew spied on the horizon a leaky, little boat. And crammed inside were refugees from Indochina hoping to get to America. The *Midway* sent a small launch to bring them to the ship and safety. As the refugees made their way through th e choppy seas, one spied the sailor on deck and stood up and called out to him. He yelled, "Hello, American sailor. Hello, freedom man."[2]

When a father mentors his son and disciplines him, he gives that young man freedom.

When a father fails to provide that discipline for his son, he robs his son of his future potential and freedom.

Cuba lost freedom when they gave up their guns.

Israel lost freedom when they gave up the blacksmith and their swords.

Your son will lose his freedom if you fail to discipline him.

So go to it, freedom man.

Until Eve arrived, this was a man's world.

—Richard Armour

CHAPTER SIX

MASCULINE SONS
IN A FEMINIZED WORLD
(MENTORING THROUGH MASCULINITY)

I LIVE IN TEXAS AND I OWN FOUR COWS.

I believe that makes me a Texas cattleman.

It all started a couple of years ago when I bought two pregnant cows. Six months later, another cow showed up. Four weeks later, a baby bull showed up. That's when life got interesting.

Before that baby bull showed up, I would walk across the pasture and the last thing on my mind was cows. But once the baby bull got about six months old, I couldn't walk across that pasture without thinking about him. That little bull thought he owned that pasture. And he didn't like me coming onto his turf. So he would charge me without warning. I used to enjoy walking across that pasture. So did my wife. But the bigger that bull got, the less I enjoyed the pasture. This little bull was too aggressive. He wouldn't be quiet and calm like the three females that shared the pasture with him. He was ruining my evening walks with his aggressiveness and willingness to do battle. He wouldn't cooperate and act like the other cows.

So I made a call to the vet.

Three days later, when I drove by the barn there were two testicles hanging from the fence. That night I walked in the pasture and the bull didn't charge me. He looked at me slightly cross-eyed but he didn't charge.

He had been castrated. He was now just like his mother. And from that day on, he has acted like his mother.

FEMINIZED

We don't castrate boys, but we certainly feminize them. And we don't even realize that we're doing it. Most of us didn't even know it was possible to feminize a boy. But it is. And to one extent or another, it has happened to every male in our culture. But the good news is that, unlike castration, it is reversible.

It's very clear that God wants fathers to mentor their sons. When a son is mentored, loved, and disciplined by a father who loves him, that boy will unconsciously learn how to be masculine. When a boy is mentored by women, or raised primarily by women, then that boy will become almost certainly feminized. But don't forget that this can be easily reversed.

So what is feminization?

Stephen Clark describes it well:

> A feminized male is a male who has learned to behave or react in ways that are more appropriate to women. The feminized male can be normal as a male, with no tendencies to reject being male and no tendencies toward homosexuality, and yet he can have been

so influenced by women or can have so identified himself with a world in which women dominate, that many of his interests and traits are more womanly than manly. Compared to men who have not been feminized, he will place much higher emphasis and attention on how he feels and how other people feel. He will be much more gentle and handle situations in a "soft" way. He will be much more subject to the approval of the group, especially emotionally expressed approval (that is, how others feel about him and what he is doing, how others react to him). He will sometimes tend to relate by preference to women and other feminized or effeminate men, and he will sometimes have a difficult time with an all-male group. He will tend to fear women's emotions, and in his family and at work can be easily controlled by the possibility of women (his mother, his wife, or co-worker) having an emotional reaction. He will tend to idealize women and, if he is religious, he will tend to see in women the ideal Christians or the definition of what it means to be spiritual. He will identify Christian virtue with feminine characteristics. . . . A feminized man may have a character in which the traits of gentleness and quietness are stronger than the traits of aggressiveness and courage.[1]

How can a boy learn to be a man if he is always with women in his formative years? The answer is he is going to have a very difficult time learning to be a man when he is constantly in the presence of women. Young boys need women who love them and care for them. Godly women can have a wonderful influence on young boys. But he needs a man in his life to show him what masculinity looks like.

Clark continues:

> Feminization is a cultural pattern passed on to men, leading them to take a feminized approach to emotions, personal relations and values. This cultural pattern is passed on through the media, the school system, and the family, and has its greatest impact in childhood and adolescence. Unlike effeminacy, feminization is not difficult to change. It mainly requires exposure to a new cultural pattern—new models, a new social environment, a new set of values.[2]

Straight out of the blocks, I can tell you that David wasn't feminized. David was a gifted musician, but he wasn't feminized. He was a man with a tender heart and he was not afraid to express his emotions—but he wasn't feminized. He was a fearless warrior and he wasn't feminized. As a boy, he single-handedly took on a bear to protect his sheep. He killed the bear and he also killed a lion. David was masculine. In his time, boys were with men. From approximately age seven, boys were raised by their fathers and older brothers. A young boy was primarily in the company of men. It was necessary because it was a rough world. At times, it was kill or be killed.

How many guys do you know who have taken on a lion with their bare hands? We live in a different world than David did. That's why feminization wasn't an issue for him, but it is for us and our sons. When David got focused later in life on the importance of mentoring, he had something to offer that is increasingly rare in our culture. He was masculine. Therefore, he had something to offer to his son that was of immense value.

Why has authentic masculinity become so rare?

It's sort of a wasp-and-spider issue.

There is a type of wasp that you want to avoid at all costs if you are an argyra spider. The type of wasp you never want to encounter is the Hymenoepimecis wasp. This wasp is a parasite. And it turns the spider into something it was never intended to be. It all begins when the wasp stings the spider.

When the stinger enters the spider, the spider is temporarily paralyzed. The wasp then lays its egg inside the abdomen of the spider. The spider soon recovers and does the normal work of a spider, which, of course, is spinning webs. The spider does this for the next ten to fourteen days while the wasp egg grows inside it. At that point, the egg secretes a chemical that forces the spider to do what the spider has never done before. Instead of spinning a web, the spider begins to build a cocoon for the unborn wasp inside its abdomen. By nature, spiders don't build cocoons; they build webs. But when the wasp penetrates the insides of the spider, the spider begins to exhibit traits that are not normal to spiders.

When the cocoon has been constructed for the unborn wasp, it kills the spider and continues to grow in the cocoon until it is born.

When the spider is so infiltrated by the wasp, the spider loses its natural purpose and begins to express behaviors that are contrary to its nature.

That's what happens to a man when he becomes feminized.

The only difference is that the man can recover his God-given purpose and function. Unfortunately, it's all over for the spider.[3]

Men in American culture have been stung by feminization. And like the spider, they don't even know it. Everything seems normal and life goes on. But things aren't normal because the man is behaving differently than God intended. That's serious. And the wasps aren't saying a word.

STEROID MASCULINITY

So what is masculinity?

It's a willingness to lead, assume responsibility, and be a self-starter. Masculine men take initiative. It's an inclination to despise passivity and do the right thing. It's a willingness to stand alone and be unpopular. It is a desire to provide and protect for one's family and those who are weak and disadvantaged. It requires courage, honor, and the willingness to sacrifice, even if necessary, one's own life for the good of others. That's masculinity.

The world thinks you're masculine if you're a street fighter. The world thinks you're masculine if you take steroids and look powerful. But those kinds of activities don't make you masculine. You can be the toughest guy on the block and biggest guy in the gym and still be feminized.

True masculinity is not valued in our culture. It is shunned and mocked. The media and the academic elite want men who have been worked on by a vet. They want only hardworking, driven men who are very, very sensitive. But when those two planes hit the Twin Towers on September 11, what we suddenly needed were masculine men. Feminized men don't walk into burning buildings. But masculine men do. That's why God created men to be masculine.

In our times, men are being feminized not only in the culture, but in the church as well. Therefore, feminization is a great danger to your son becoming the man that God wants him to be.

A truly masculine man honors God and blesses all who are led by him. There are great illustrations of masculinity throughout Scripture. Shadrach, Meshach, and Abednego, who walked into a fiery inferno. Daniel who faced the hungry lions in a dark den. Joseph who fled from the wife of Potiphar. David's dearest friend, Jonathan, who died fighting valiantly for the righteous cause of his God. Joshua who fought mightily the great pagan giants of Canaan, and beat them soundly by the help of his Commander in Chief. The apostles Paul and Peter, and all of the thousands of disciples who died martyrs' deaths for the good name of Christ and the cause of truth.

Sadly, many of the Old Testament kings abandoned masculinity out of fear—fear of other more powerful kingdoms and foes, fear that God really wouldn't come through on his promises, fear of bodily harm, fear of a loss of power upon the throne, fear of a woman like Jezebel and Athaliah, her daughter, who had their own devious ways of emasculating men. These kings simply didn't have the testicles to be real men when it was real men that were needed.

King David was an exception. And David modeled that masculinity for Solomon.

In the gut of every man beats a masculine heart. It needs only a jump-start to get that heart pumping. God made you to be masculine. He wants you to experience the joy of masculinity in all its fullness and pleasure. But men must begin by stepping forward and saying yes to him and no to the feminized world in which we live. And when we do that, our sons are just a step behind us, copying our every move.

THE CAUSE OF FEMINIZATION

Feminization has different symptoms, just as heart disease has different symptoms. Let me underscore two points that Stephen Clark made earlier. A feminized male is not the same as a man who is effeminate. A feminized male is not a man who is attracted to other men. Feminization is subtler than that. It has to do with the fact that for most of us, women have been the dominant persons in our lives.

Marion J. Levy Jr. describes just how serious the problem really is:

> Our young males are the first people of whom the following
> can be said: if they are males, they and their fathers and their brothers
> and sons and all the males they know are overwhelmingly likely to
> have been reared under the direct domination of females from birth
> to maturity. No less important is the fact that their mothers and their
> sisters and their girlfriends and their wives and all of the ladies with
> whom they have to do have had to do only with males so reared.
> Most of us have not even noticed this change, nor do we have any
> realization of its radicality. We certainly do not have any systematic
> body of speculation on what the significance of so radical a change is
> or could be. To put the matter as dramatically as possible, we do not
> even know whether viable human beings can over any long period of
> time be reared in such a fashion. After all, this has never held true of
> any substantial proportion of any population for even one generation
> in the history of the world until the last fifty years.[4]

If you have any question about this, let me ask you, how many of
your teachers between kindergarten and sixth grade were male? We
have developed a system where the primary influence upon boys, Mon-
day through Friday, five days a week, is women teachers. Now in the
vast majority of cases, these women teachers have the best of intentions
toward their male students. But that's not the issue. The issue is that we
put boys in a system for forty hours a week with women instead of men.

When you were in elementary school, did one of your female
teachers ever send a note home to your parents alerting them to the fact

that you wouldn't sit still in class? That happened to me on a regular basis. As a matter of fact, when I was in fourth grade I was sent to the principal's office usually once a day. Not for being disrespectful, but for not sitting still.

Let me ask you a question. Did almighty God create eight-year-old boys to sit still behind a desk inside a room for eight hours a day? If you are a man, you say no. If you are a woman, you may say yes.

And when a boy is with women who want him to act like the little girls who do sit still for eight hours a day and don't breathe, what kind of behavior are they going to reinforce? The women teachers are going to reward the boys and give them good grades for conduct when the boy begins to act like a girl in the system. That's one way boys get feminized. But it's bigger than that.

When a boy is with women constantly and continually, hour after hour, day after day, week after week, month after month, year after year, and only occasionally is with his father or some other male figure, who is going to influence him the most? That's easy. Do you see how a normal male who is not effeminate and not attracted sexually to other males can be feminized?

THE CURE FOR FEMINIZATION

The cause of feminization in a man's life is that he is primarily in the presence of women rather than men. The cure for feminization is for that male to be with other males who are not feminized. And what better place to begin than in the church of Christ?

Our sons need to be around masculine preaching and worship.

They need to see masculine men in our pulpits, preaching like the masculine messengers of the Bible. We need Elijahs and John the

Baptists, who are unafraid to speak boldly against a godless culture and call sin what it is. We need Isaiahs and Jeremiahs who will speak in the political arenas and courts of the land. These guys could look a king straight in the eye and tell him the truth. They had no problem proclaiming judgment on behalf of the great Judge. Their goal was repentance, revival, and a return to the God of our salvation. Yet today the trend is to soften our message and feminize our leaders. Of late, judgment of sin has become religiously incorrect. The greatest offense has become that of offending. But truth by its very nature is offensive to those who are living in sin. Satan hates the truth. And he'll do anything to prevent it from being proclaimed.

Gentlemen, we are at war. Ephesians 6 says we are in a battle more gruesome and significant than any physical battle on earth. When was the last time you heard a sermon on the importance of being a warrior for righteousness, or being aggressive in telling the truth regardless of the cost? More often the traits we hear uplifted are the more *feminine traits:* tenderness, compassion, sensitivity, gentleness. Are these important traits? Yes they are. Are they more spiritual or desirable than aggressiveness, courage, and standing on truth? No they are not. In this war between good and evil, against Satan and his demons, we need "tender warriors." But the trend today is to major on the "tender" and minor on the "warrior." So our pulpits have increasingly become a place of finesse, soft-balling, dumbing down, attempting not to offend.

May I be so frank as to say that in the trenches you don't want tenderness? You want passionate and courageous warriors—men willing to die if need be for the cause. We have lost bold, truth-centered, masculine preaching, and it's killing our congregations.

Feminized Worship

What about our worship? I do a lot of traveling and speak in churches all over the country. And I have observed a trend that disturbs me. It is a trend towards soft, feminine worship. Now, I have friends whom I respect and appreciate who are involved in leading churches with this approach. I don't question their heart or their motives. They want to honor Christ. But someone is influencing the concept of worship in a way that needs to be challenged. I wonder if this approach to worship has been thought through and evaluated biblically. I want to describe the kind of worship that I am seeing as the latest trend. I think it is counterproductive because it is feminized. See what you think.

In many cases, the guy who is leading the worship is very soft-spoken, quiet, and passive. He may or may not be that way offstage—but up front, that's the demeanor that is considered "spiritual."

When he prays, he prays softly. He doesn't lead out in prayer; he puts you to sleep in prayer. The style is one of devoted hesitation. The words are very halting. It's all very nonconfrontational.

Where is the confidence in prayer?

Hebrews 4:16 lays it out there: "Therefore, let us draw near with confidence to the throne of grace, so that we may receive mercy and find grace to help in time of need."

And then, when it's time to sing, they turn down the lights. Why do they turn down the lights? They are trying to establish a mood. Let me make an observation here. The worship of almighty God is not based on mood; it is based on truth.

Then to keep the mood going they sing the same chorus over and over and over and over and over. I was a guest in a church recently and they kept singing, "I could sing of your love forever." And I actually thought they were going to.

I noticed the breakdown of the service. They took forty-five minutes setting the mood in worship. Then I was given not quite thirty minutes to teach the Scriptures. When the message was over, they got up and sang for ten more minutes. That's fifty-five minutes setting the mood and twenty-five minutes for teaching truth.

Something is seriously wrong here.

Can you imagine the prophets of the Old Testament in a place like this? Can you imagine David, or Peter, or Jeremiah in a setting like this?

In the Old Testament, they didn't turn down the lights and set a mood. They slit the throats of animals, poured out their blood, gutted their intestines, and burned them in the fire. The sacrificial system is no longer with us because the Lord Jesus was the Lamb of God who took away the sins of the world. But there was reality in that worship and it was centered in the truth that sin is terrible and horrible and that forgiveness of sin is not cheap. Mel Gibson did us all a service when he reenacted the terrible suffering that Christ went through to secure our salvation. It wasn't soft and it didn't set a mood. That movie made you want to throw up at points because of the horrific suffering that Christ went through for us. You had a deep sense of worship in your mind and heart of what it cost Christ to be the Lamb of God who paid for my sin by his sacrifice.

These contemporary "worship" atmospheres are weak. So is it my opinion that we should only sing hymns? No. Let's sing worship choruses, but let's make sure they have biblical content. The present trend gives the wrong impression of Christianity. A setting like that is feminine. A setting like that is for women. And it all seems so spiritual. But it isn't. Am I in a church or a spa? At a deal like that you don't bring your Bible; you bring your moisturizer.

And one more thing. It turns men off and it turns them away. Young boys sit in a setting like that and think it's weird; therefore, God must be weird. God isn't weird. He is so great and powerful that He is to be feared. Now that's a God worth serving.

Shampoo and Conditioner

Yes, the church has even feminized the Lord Jesus Christ.

That's why I get so tired of songs that speak over and over of the "beauty" of Christ. The apostles never said he was beautiful, so why should we? There is beauty to his character, but that distinction is rarely made. The impression of his "beauty" that is given today is feminine. But Christ was male, not female. One doesn't compliment a man by saying that he is beautiful. The appropriate word in that context would be "handsome." If you went up to John Wayne and said he was beautiful, he would separate several of your molars and bicuspids into a new world order. But if you said he was handsome, he would tip his hat and thank you for the kind word. If you were a woman, that is.

Let's stop describing Jesus Christ in womanly terms. He is awesome, majestic, holy, and righteous. He is the Son of the Living God. He is the God/man. Let's show Him the proper respect and use masculine, biblical terms to describe his greatness. And in the process, we won't be sending a wrong message about his person and character.

When I was a kid, women's magazines would often have an ad on the back cover for Breck Shampoo that would feature a new "Breck girl" each month. It was a portrait of a beautiful young woman with lustrous hair. The woman in the portrait would have a flawless complexion and long, flowing, shiny, lustrous hair. I remember seeing these when my mom's magazines would come in the mail.

I also remember when I was about five or six, going with my mom to a Christian bookstore. Hanging over the door was a very famous picture of Jesus kneeling in prayer at the Garden of Gethsemane.

I noticed his hands, and they were silky smooth. He had no calluses. His fingernails almost looked manicured. His complexion was flawless. He looked liked he moisturized without fail. And his hair. His hair was unbelievable. Shiny, lustrous, and full, it swept down his shoulders with just the right amount of wave and panache. I looked at that picture of Jesus as a five-year-old kid, and I thought to myself, *Breck girl*. Jesus looked just like the Breck girl.

On perhaps two different occasions, the Lord Jesus walked into the temple with a whip and commenced to drive out the commodity traders that had managed to extort office space in his Father's house.

And when he walked into that temple with that whip and started turning over tables, they didn't say, "Look at his hair! I wonder who does his nails?"

What they said was "Where the heck is the nearest exit?"

Whoever painted that picture that I saw in the Christian bookstore had it all wrong. He must have painted that picture with the lights down low and a candle glowing in the background because he completely missed what Jesus looked like.

Jesus was raised by Joseph in the carpenter's shop and he didn't buy his lumber at Home Depot. He cut his own trees and planed his own boards. As a result, he had some serious forearms. And he didn't have soft hands. He had calluses from doing hard, physical labor. That's why they ran when he cleared out the temple. No one stood up to him. That's because he didn't look like the painting in the Christian bookstore.

If you've got that picture hanging somewhere, get rid of it. You wouldn't want your son to get the wrong idea about the King of Kings. If you have any doubts about what Jesus really looks like, we have an eye-witness description from the apostle John when he was exiled on Patmos. Read this description of Christ that is recorded in Revelation 19:11–16, as he returns to the earth for the second time, and read it slowly:

> And I saw heaven opened, and behold, a white horse, and He who sat on it is called Faithful and True, and in righteousness He judges and wages war.
>
> His eyes are a flame of fire, and on His head are many diadems; and He has a name written on Him which no one knows except Himself.
>
> He is clothed with a robe dipped in blood, and his name is called The Word of God.
>
> And the armies which are in heaven, clothed in fine linen, white and clean, were following Him on white horses.
>
> From His mouth comes a sharp sword, so that with it He may strike down the nations, and He will rule them with a rod of iron; and He treads the wine press of the fierce wrath of God, the Almighty.
>
> And on His robe and on His thigh He has a name written, "KING OF KINGS, AND LORD OF LORDS."

I didn't see anything in there about shampoo or moisturizers. And John never mentions that Christ was beautiful. So let's learn from a man who actually saw Him. And let us not sin by misrepresenting Him to our sons.

JOIN THE CLUB

Years ago, a great hunter was walking through a jungle in Africa. He came into a clearing and was startled to see a huge rhinoceros lying dead in the grass. As he walked around to the other side of the massive animal he was even more startled to see a Pygmy.

"Did you just kill this rhino?" asked the hunter.

"Yes, I did," said the Pygmy proudly.

"I don't mean to be offensive, but how could a small man kill such a large animal?"

"I killed it with my club," responded the Pygmy.

"That's incredible. How big is your club?"

The Pygmy paused and said, "There's about one hundred of us in the club."

There's another club of men that I want to mention to you. And unless I miss my guess, you are already in the club. If not, you can join up right now. The club to which I refer is comprised of men who want to mentor masculine sons. Joining this club requires a commitment to providing an example of masculinity and encouraging masculinity in your son's life. There are a number of ways to go about that. I mention several to get you started.

To defeat feminization and encourage masculine behavior you must:

- *assume your God-appointed post as head of your family*
- *teach your son to stand alone*
- *consider the school alternatives*
- *read Louis L'Amour westerns (no kidding)*

Let's break these down one by one.

Assume Your God-Appointed Post as Head of Your Family

Every family has a chief. In your extended family, are the chiefs men or are they women? In the home in which you were raised, was your dad the chief or was it your mom? I am not talking about the "domestic rule" of making a home, which is to be delegated to the wife by her husband and commanded by God to be her rightful reign (see 1 Timothy 5:14). I am talking about leadership of the home and the headship of the home.

If you come from a home where your father gave up his role as tribal chief to your mother, don't you do that. You are the head, you are the leader, and you will answer to God. And if you give up that role to your wife, you will have to explain that to the Lord.

Let me shoot very straight with you if you have given up your post to your wife. You cannot continue to do that. It is sin. You are violating God's clear command to you (Ephesians 5; Titus 2; 1 Timothy 2–3; 1 Peter 3). He wants you to do this and to do it unto Him. You cannot mentor your son if you allow a strong woman to run your home.

Those who know your family well know who the chief is. Your kids know it, your wife knows it, and you know it. If you have given it up, without making a scene or calling a press conference, just simply begin to take it back. Don't announce that you are going to lead—just begin to do it. Honor your wife, love your wife, and consider carefully her input. But do not be nagged into violating your conscience. Do not give in to subtle and sometimes not-so-subtle female manipulations in order to keep the peace.

When men give in to keep the peace, rather than dealing with the dysfunction, they never get peace. You don't need that in your family. Nobody needs it. You don't need it, your son doesn't need it, and your daughter doesn't need it. Love your wife but don't let her play you like a violin. If she is running you, then you have allowed her to feminize you.

If she notices a difference, then great. Most women long for such godly, masculine leadership. They respect it immensely and desire it more than you know. Most women will respond to this in a positive way. But if she is disturbed because she has enjoyed the position and she likes being the chief, just lovingly tell her that you love her too much to let this continue. You are going to love her as Christ loves the church—sacrificially, respectfully, and giving her all the dignity that she deserves. But you are going to lead—for her sake and the sake of the children and ultimately because Christ has commanded you to do so. You are going to yield to Christ, not to her. And if you must say this, say it as honorably as you can. This is an obedience issue for a man. Are you going to obey your Lord or is your wife going to manipulate you out of it?

You must become the spiritual leader of your family. If you do not do this, I tell you straight up that you have feminized yourself. Step up and be the man you want to be in your heart and fulfill your divine responsibility. This is what your wife and kids desperately need. So how do you do that? Several years ago I wrote a book titled *Point Man*, for men who want to become better spiritual leaders for their families. If this is where you are, then you may find that book helpful. I can't cover that material here. I can only tell you here that you must do this to stop the feminization of men in your family. You can't raise your son to be a family leader if you aren't doing it. And you can do it. Even if you don't have a clue where to begin, as you look at Christ and follow carefully his instructions to husbands, he will immediately begin to transform the feminization right out of your life. The more like Christ we become the more masculine we are.

One of our greatest presidents was Theodore Roosevelt. A president is a chief. And Teddy Roosevelt was not only a great chief for the nation; he was a great chief for his family. He understood that leadership must be modeled.

> Roosevelt was convinced that leadership could not exist in isolation. Leadership had to be modeled after some tangible, practical, and realizable ideal. Thus, all great leaders were, in truth, simply students of men of unimpeachable character, unreproachable courage, and unswerving vision. Leaders had mentors. They were disciples. Rather than striking out as lonely pioneers, they were willing to stand on the shoulders of those who had gone before....
>
> Thus, he never attempted to escape from the shadow of his father. He never tried to establish an independent reputation for himself. Instead, he always felt that he was accountable to a kind of family trust and a national covenant.[5]

This great president learned to be a chief by modeling himself after the example of his own father. In his own words, President Theodore Roosevelt said of his father:

> I have a special sense of that great legacy, being the son of the finest man, the happiest man, I have ever known. He showed me what it means to live for right. He was a living illustration of the American ideal and spirit. All that I have ever done has been little more than an attempt to live up to and honor that legacy.[6]

Theodore Roosevelt was an extremely busy man, but he was never too busy for his children. He wrote thousands of letters to his children in his lifetime. Even when he was away from home, he was working to connect. When he was leading men into battle at San Juan Hill, his bravery and steadiness under fire would prove to be an example to his sons. His leadership in that battle would make him the most famous man in America. Yet his heart and integrity were captured by a short statement that he penned in a letter: "Better faithful than famous." [7]

He was the most famous man on earth, but that meant nothing to him. What mattered to him was faithfulness. Family chiefs and commanders in chief are to model masculinity and selflessness to those they lead. And with that, Teddy Roosevelt leads us to our next principle.

Teach Your Son to Stand Alone

If you know anything at all about the life of President Theodore Roosevelt, it would be that he was a man who was willing to stand alone. He would rather be faithful to God, his family, and his principles than anything else in life.

His four sons learned that principle from the example of their father. Ted Jr., Kermit, Archie, and Quentin all proved under enemy fire that they were willing to be faithful and stand alone regardless of the cost.

And this came out when they went to war to serve their country.

In January 1918, Kermit Roosevelt, serving with the British forces in the Middle East, broke down the door of a house. He suspected several soldiers were lying in ambush. He was wrong. The entire house was filled with Turkish soldiers. He was all alone. Kermit was shocked but quickly got his bearings and confidently demanded their immediate surrender. The startled Turks threw down their arms and did precisely that. For his bravery, Kermit was awarded the British Army Cross.[8] Kermit

Roosevelt was not a feminized young man.

That same year, Archie was hit by an exploding German shell. The doctors were on the verge of amputating his leg, when he began to take a turn for the better. They saved his leg, but he would be crippled for the rest of his life. For his heroism, he was awarded the Croix de Guerre by the French army.[9]

1918 was proving to be a difficult year for the Roosevelt sons. On July 14, 1918, Quentin was with his squadron over Germany in a classic dogfight, when he spotted another German squadron sneaking in from behind. Single-handedly, he turned and took on the enemy squadron. He was willing to stand alone to save the lives of his fellow pilots. But it cost him his life as the overwhelming firepower shot him out of the sky.

That leaves one more son, Ted Jr. Not only was Ted Jr. wounded in World War I, but he was the most decorated soldier in all of World War II. At the age of fifty-six, he was the only general to go in with the first wave of soldiers at Normandy Beach on D-Day. Recovering from pneumonia, and hiding his angina from the doctors, he did everything he could do to land on the beach first. He walked with a cane and he was told that no generals would go in with the first wave. Yet he felt that the young lads facing the Nazi bullets might be encouraged to see him go with them. So he did.

For hours "he stood out in the open with bullets whistling by him, waving his cane, calmly sending troops to their assignments. So conspicuous was his courage that it would become legendary within hours, traveling by word of mouth along the beaches."[10] His own young son, also named Ted, was among the boys hitting the beaches, but he didn't know where. All he knew was that when everyone else was crawling on their bellies, someone needed to stand and give them direction. That's why General George S. Patton said that Ted Jr. was the bravest soldier he had ever known. He was willing to stand alone.

Twenty-five days later the fifty-six-year-old general who had survived Normandy was reunited with his son who had also survived. He admitted to his son that he had been experiencing severe chest pains. His son urged him to see the doctor but just hours later he died of a heart attack. He was buried on July 14, 1944. It was twenty-six years to the day after his brother Quentin had been shot down over France.[11] For his bravery, Theodore Roosevelt Jr., the son of a great president, was awarded posthumously the Medal of Honor.

Fours sons willing to stand alone. They were not feminized young men. They loved life and they loved their families. But they learned from the example of their father, who had led men into battle on San Juan Hill and stood for truth all of his life, that sometimes a man must stand alone and sacrifice.

Have your sons ever seen you take a stand?

Are you willing to stand up and be counted when it might cost you something? The most cherished truths of the Bible are under attack in our day. Are you willing to stand up and speak against the slaughter of innocent babies and the perversion of "marriage" between couples of the same sex?

Psalm 15 describes what a man of godly integrity is like. In verse 4, a godly man is described as "in whose eyes a reprobate is despised, but who honors those who fear the Lord."

A reprobate is someone who is opposed to God, His laws, and His truth. He lives in outright rebellion and defiance before God. Our culture tells us to approve of these people. The Scriptures say they are to be despised. Most of us find that a little too strong but it comes directly from the Word of God.

Do you despise people like this, or do you vote for them? Do you have the courage to speak against them, or do you keep your thoughts to yourself because you don't want to offend anyone? Feminized men need the approval of the group. They want to be popular. Your son will struggle with popularity. Let him know that it is more important to you that he is respected than that he is popular. That's the mark of a leader and that's the mark of masculinity. So show him what it looks like. These reprobates are people, and they need Christ. But someone needs to have the courage to tell the truth and offer the only One who can save their lives.

Consider the School Alternatives

This one is short and sweet. Not only does your son need a good education, but he also needs healthy interaction with males as a part of that education. On both counts, the public schools are woefully inadequate. Educationally, the public school system is deficient in biblical truth. And it is predominately female. So what are the options?

Home-schooling is an option. And perhaps you can teach your son a subject or two. Or you can find a co-op home-school situation where different parents share the teaching load. I know dads who are good at math who teach the math class. They don't do it full-time because they don't need to do it full-time.

There are also Christian schools that offer "classic" curriculums that actually educate students. Once again, you are going to find more male teachers in a classical school situation. That male presence is important.

We will say more about education in the upcoming chapters in this book. But for now, let me say that whatever decision you make about your son's education, notice the men that will surround him. Get to know them. And make sure you are involved in what he is learning and experiencing at school. A father's involvement in his son's education is rare these days, and utterly refreshing.

Read Louis L'Amour Westerns

What did President Dwight Eisenhower, President Ronald Reagan, and Coach Tom Landry all have in common? They were all Louis L'Amour fans.

Coach Landry had a ritual that he followed after every Dallas Cowboy road game. Win or lose, he would get on the team plane, pull out a Louis L'Amour paperback, and read it all the way home.

L'Amour died in 1988, but he wrote over 100 books that have sold over 250 million copies. That's a lot of books. L'Amour is popular because he wrote about masculine men who believed in right and wrong. They made their own way, provided for their families, protected women and children, and faced off enemies. They were men in an age when a man did what was necessary.

L'Amour writes great, clean stories that are well-crafted and celebrate masculinity. Pick up one and read it and you'll be hooked. Many of his books are on audiotape. We have many fond memories of driving the interstate from Texas to California, listening to great stories of Louis L'Amour about the men who built the West.

By the way, do you know how many masculine men it takes to change a lightbulb? The answer is none. Masculine men don't change lightbulbs. Masculine men aren't afraid of the dark.

And that's no bull.

It is not good for a man to pray cream and live skim milk.

—HENRY WARD BEECHER

CHAPTER SEVEN

WHY YOUR SON EXISTS

(MENTORING THROUGH GUIDANCE)

EDDIE COULDN'T BELIEVE HIS OWN SUCCESS. HE LIVED IN A GATED, secure mansion in one of the most exclusive sections of Chicago. He drove new cars, ate in the best restaurants, and traveled in style. Servants took care of the estate and the grounds. His wife and children had the very best of everything. Eddie was a brilliant attorney who had succeeded beyond his wildest dreams. There was just one problem. He was crooked.

Eddie's only client was the notorious gangster Al Capone. It was Eddie who kept Capone out of jail. Eddie was personally sickened by the violence and murders, but he was in too far to ever back out.

Eddie had a young son whom he loved with all his heart. He wanted the very best for his boy. His son was a natural leader with a love for life. His young son worshiped his dad and respected him with every ounce of his being. But Eddie knew one day that respect would be lost. That's what kept eating at him. And eventually it was the factor that caused him to make the decision that would cost him his life. Eddie wanted a better life for his son. So he decided to do the only thing he could do to get back his integrity. He went to the police and told them the truth. It was Eddie who gave the IRS all of Capone's financial records. With that information, Capone was finished.

But so was Eddie. Just months after doing the right thing, he died in a blaze of machine gun fire on a Chicago street. But he died leaving his son an example of doing the right thing—no matter what the cost. He wanted to give his son a better life. He wanted to prepare his son to handle the challenges that he would one day face in life. It was the hardest decision that he ever made. But it was the best decision he ever made.

I'm in airports quite a bit. And I often find myself going through the busiest airport in the world, O'Hare International in Chicago. There is a small memorial, located between two of the terminals, built to the memory of Butch O'Hare. Butch O'Hare was the first ace of World War II and the first naval aviator to be awarded the Congressional Medal of Honor.

This young pilot was out on a mission with his squadron when he noticed that his fuel was dangerously low. Apparently, someone had made a mistake and not topped off his fuel tank. He radioed his flight commander and was ordered to return to the ship. As he was doing so, he saw in the distance a squadron of Japanese fighters headed toward the American fleet. Unable to warn the fleet of the coming attack, he turned his plane into the Japanese squadron, firing with everything he had.

Flying in and out of the Japanese squadron, he picked off plane after plane until he was out of ammunition. Then he dove into the wing or tail of a plane, attempting to disable it from attacking the fleet. The Japanese squadron cut off the attack and turned back. It was a miracle that Butch was able to return to the ship. And it had all been captured on the gun camera that recorded the entire event. Butch had taken out five enemy fighter planes.

A year later, Butch died in another dogfight. This courageous young man, in the prime of life, died in a blaze of bullets that throttled his plane and his body. Butch O'Hare died that day just as his father had died before him in a torrent of bullets on a cold Chicago street. Butch O'Hare died a hero. And so did his father, Eddie O'Hare. It was the courage of his father in standing against evil that gave him a mission and purpose in life to do the same.

It is the job of a father to prepare his son for life. Even if it costs you your life.

A FATHER'S HEART

David had the same desire for his son as Eddie O'Hare had for his. David wanted to give Solomon what he needed to prepare him for life and for leadership.

That's why David showed Solomon from the time he was a little guy what it was to be a man's man—a "tender warrior" (to use Stu Weber's great book title) who could express his emotions openly, love and praise God passionately, and fight to the death on behalf of God's truth and honor.

If this had been all David did, Solomon would have been fortunate. But David did something more. He gave one of the greatest blessings a father can ever give to his son. David gave Solomon a very clear sense of purpose—or "calling"—or "mission" in his life. Every son wants and desires a very clear purpose. And that's where a father comes in. It's your job to help him discover why God has put him on the earth. You don't have all the answers and neither do I. But as we walk with the Lord he will give us the wisdom that we need to mentor our sons and get them ready for life.

So what is it that a son needs from his father?

- *A son needs purpose*
- *A son needs a plan*
- *A son needs patience*
- *A son needs a path*

A SON NEEDS PURPOSE

A young boy whose father believes that he has a unique purpose in life can go to the moon and back on that belief. I'm not talking about a dad who says, "You will be great." That's egotistical. And it focuses his son on the wrong thing. It focuses on his son's need for *success*, instead of his need to *discover his God-ordained purpose and calling*. Did you catch that difference? The last thing your son needs is the pressure to be some great success out there in the world. What he needs is to know that God has created him for a purpose, and if he follows the Lord with his whole heart, he will discover that purpose.

For most of his adult life, J. Paul Getty was the richest man on the face of the earth. He was fabulously wealthy and successful. Getty had four sons, Paul, Gordon, Ronald, and his eldest, George.

A close family friend, Stuart Evey, wrote that "over the years, J. Paul Getty felt no need to be a father to his sons, and it showed in them."[1]

As a young man, J. Paul Getty's son Paul would write letters to his absent father, longing to be close to him. The letters would come back with his spelling and grammatical errors corrected by his father. There was no personal reply from the father. Paul later became a heroin addict.

Gordon's primary interaction with his father was in court and handled by attorneys. Of course, the issue was money.

When Ronald decided to pursue his interest in making films, his father ridiculed him.

George worked under his father's stern gaze in the family oil business. He took his own life by stabbing himself in the stomach and taking an overdose of pills.

Here were four young men who lived in a prison of their father's success. But he never enabled them to discover their purpose.

J. Paul Getty was a success at success but a failure as a father.

It is the task of a father to help his son find his unique purpose in life. When a dad believes in his son in this way, he has done something almost sacred. It's as if he has put his hand of blessing upon his son's head, just as Abraham blessed Isaac, and Isaac in turn blessed Jacob.

Your son was born for a purpose. He is not here by accident. God made him just the way he is, absolutely unique. Is he autistic or physically handicapped? He is here for a purpose. Is he shy and retiring? He is here for a purpose. Is he strong-willed and difficult to handle? He is here for a purpose. In his uniqueness, God has something for your son to do. There is a reason that he exists.

If you teach him this from his earliest days, he will rise up to that calling. Here is what goes on in his mind under the surface: "My dad is on my team. He doesn't pressure me to be someone else. My dad likes the way that God wired me and he believes that God has a purpose for my life."

When your son picks that up from you, you have set him free. He doesn't have to be something he's not.

So what is God's purpose for your son? Only God knows that. But when God has something special for someone to do, he gives them the equipment that they need to accomplish that purpose. Another way of saying it is that God puts "gifts" or "bents" or "assets" into a child. As that child grows and matures, those bents will become apparent. And those bents, those assets, will one day be used by God in enabling him to fulfill his destiny and purpose.

David built into Solomon a sense of destiny. He recognized his teachable spirit before the Lord, his innate wisdom, and his visionary bent. And David had an added word from the Lord God himself. God declared to David that Solomon would have a high calling, which he was gifted to fulfill. He would not only rule well upon the throne, but he would build the temple which would be like no other temple on earth and which would bring the greatest honor to the Lord.

You don't have that much information about what God wants to do through your son. Neither do I. But that doesn't mean that we can't help him in a significant way.

HIS PURPOSE AND HIS GIFTS

If you will help your son discover his God-given gifts, then you are helping him to ultimately discover his purpose. God gives men the gifts that they need to accomplish His purpose in their lives. Think of it this way: Gifts are hints of what God has in mind for your son.

There are three simple ways that a man can help his son discover his gifts:

- *First*, it's something he loves doing.
- *Second*, it comes naturally to him. *That doesn't mean he won't have to work hard to develop and hone it, but the natural ability is already there.*
- *And third*, other people will notice and point it out to him.

It may become clear to you that your son loves to read. That love for reading is not there by accident. It is there by design. So make it a point to put good books into his hands.

He may love building with Legos...morning, noon, and night. Lego cities, Lego fleets of ships, Lego machines never yet conceived by man, entire Lego continents. Don't ignore that bent. Encourage it. (It could one day help pay for your retirement!)

He may enjoy math, or have a real interest in rocks and geology. Nurture that. The world needs men of math and science who know their Creator and have the biblical foundation and insight to handle the ethical curveballs that are hurtling directly our way.

He may love to set up soldiers in battle formations. Winston Churchill spent hours doing that when he was a little boy. That was a hint of what was in his heart and what his purpose would ultimately be. If your son loves to do this, that is very good. We always need generals who serve the King of Kings. Maybe he's a crisis person—he likes the thrill of taking hold and saving lives. Encourage that.

Or maybe he's quiet and thinks... not an up-front kind of guy at all. The world is in desperate need of men who have actually thought things through well from a biblical worldview and in quietness and contentment can articulate those thoughts well. Nurture that. Feed that.

You get the gist of what I'm saying.

Here's the big-time clue about his God-given strengths. When he is functioning in an area of strength, he is motivated. He is happy. He is smiling. That's the big-time hint. And when he's not motivated or happy or smiling, that's another hint. In other words, if he doesn't enjoy piano lessons and isn't pumped at accomplishing and excelling and performing well, then don't make him take lessons for three years. That's nuts. What does he like to do? Get him going into something he enjoys. There's enough drudgery in life without making him take piano lessons because Grandma hopes he will be another Beethoven, or because you want to put him through one of your own little hoops. Our sons have enough pressure to be disciplined outside of our homes at things they find irrelevant and basically hate. Why not allow your son to have the joy of learning discipline while doing something he loves?

If he's not like you, don't try to make him be just like you. Respect the fact that God has outfitted your son with particular interests and gifts. That's going to be harder for you than it would be if he were just like you. But understand that there is a purpose in that. God has a reason he made your son different, and your job is to help him discover it.

HIS PURPOSE AND HIS SMARTS

Is school difficult for him? Does he love to work with his hands? Then encourage that. There are more kinds of smart than the smarts of academia. In his book 7 *Kinds of Smart*, Thomas Armstrong points out that schools measure only two kinds of intelligence.[2] Schools measure through books and exams and SAT scores. And it's a crying shame that so much pressure and esteem in our sons' world is on these two kinds of intelligence. It leads our sons to think that if they don't excel at the kind of intelligence that is measured in school, they are not smart at all.

Nothing could be further from the truth.

So what are the different areas of intelligence? Here are some obvious ones:

- *Word smart is obviously the ability to do well in the world of spelling, writing, and telling a story on paper or verbally.*
- *Math smart is the another obvious kind of intelligence that revolves around numbers. Mathematics is logical and rational. The ability to work with numbers can get you to the moon, program a computer, and do your taxes correctly.*

Word smart and math smart are the two primary areas that schools are focused on. But there are other kinds of smart that are just as important.[3]

- *Music smart is the ability to create and interpret music. Martin Luther used to say that next to theology, music is God's greatest gift to the church.*
- *Visual smart is working with pictures and concepts. Architects, artists, and photographers are just a few examples of those who are bent toward visual smart.*
- *Muscle smart is the ability and talent to use one's body skillfully and strategically. Finish carpenters, athletes, mechanics, surgeons, and personal trainers function in this area of intelligence. Glassblowers and body shop repairmen are artists who use their muscles to create and restore beauty.*
- *People smart is just what it says. It's an intelligence that is wired to work with people. It includes the ability to "read" people and get inside them and know what is really motivating them.*

I'm writing this chapter on my laptop in my study at home. I am sitting at a desk that was built for me by a local finish carpenter. There is a slight background noise at this moment. It's a Mozart piece that I can barely hear from the CD player in the kitchen.

The guy who built my desk asked me how in the world someone could write a book. I asked him how anyone could take some lumber and build a desk. He can't write books and I can't build desks. I also have absolutely no idea how this laptop works. But someone does. But I imagine that the guy who could fix this computer probably couldn't write a concerto like Mozart. He can write a software program but he can't write music. You get the point.

For sheer lack of time and space, I can't pursue this any further. But another excellent source on this subject is William Beausay's book *Boys! Shaping Ordinary Boys into Extraordinary Men*.[4] Just know this. There are many remarkable forms of intelligence that our modern school system virtually bypasses and ignores. And your son may possess one or more of them.

A SON NEEDS A PLAN

Solomon was fortunate in his early years because God had laid out a clear plan for him that he gave to his father, David. That plan was very simple. Solomon was to build a temple for the Lord in Jerusalem. That was the mission. But in order to pull it off, Solomon was going to need a plan. And that's where David played a huge role.

Some have suggested that this mission was sort of forced on Solomon by David and that David was somehow trying to live his life through Solomon. But the Bible is clear that this was never the intent of David. David wanted to build the temple himself. But the Lord said no.

The Lord specifically told David that it was *His* plan that Solomon should build the temple (1 Chronicles 22:7– 9). And while David passed on this mission from the very words of God to his son, Solomon clearly aspired to this mission. He embraced it as his own noble and honorable calling. You can read it for yourself in 1 Kings 1–2:12; 1 Chronicles 22:5–19; 28:2 –29:25; and 2 Chronicles 1:7–13.

Once the temple was completed, Solomon's mission was not finished. And he knew that from the start. The Bible makes this clear. Solomon was to follow after the commands of God and never turn to the right or the left (see 2 Kings 22:2). He was to lead the nation well. David impressed upon Solomon this *greatest* part of his mission, and Solomon embraced it.

Sons don't always decide to follow after the Lord. And when they choose against the Lord, it breaks their father's heart. The apostle John said, "I have no greater joy than this, to hear of my children walking in the truth" (3 John 4). And there is no greater grief than when they don't. A son who lives his life in rebellion to you and the Lord cannot discover significance and meaning for his life.

Solomon embraced the Lord and His purpose without reservation. And that had to thrill David's heart after all of the heartbreak he had experienced. If there be any doubt, here is the telling factor. When God appeared to Solomon and offered to grant to him whatever he wanted as king of Israel (2 Chronicles 1:7), Solomon could have asked for anything. He could have asked for peace from his enemies. He could have asked for a long, successful, rich, honorable life (v. 11). Instead, Solomon replied, "I am but a little child; I do not know how to go out or come in... *Give me now wisdom and knowledge,* that I may go out and come in before this people, for who can rule this great people of Yours?"

(1 Kings 3:7 and 2 Chronicles 1:10, italics mine). This request of young Solomon tells us his true heart. Solomon aspired to the calling to rule wisely and well. *In other words, he wanted to fulfill his God-given purpose instead of pursuing the ultimate emptiness of "success."*

That is significant. He wanted to rule this people wisely and well, so that he could fulfill his calling before the Lord.

God was so pleased with Solomon's request that he gave him not only the wisdom he asked for, but also everything else that he did not ask for!

To sum it up, we can say without hesitation that David wisely mentored Solomon in recognizing his gifts and discovering his calling. Go and do likewise with your boy.

A SON NEEDS PATIENCE

Wouldn't it be nice if God would communicate as clearly to us about our sons as He did to David about Solomon? It would certainly help if God were to say, "I want your son to discover a cure for hemophilia by the time he is forty." But God doesn't do that. Yet, he still has a purpose. God will make it clear in his time. So in the interim, it's going to take some patience. But that's okay, because God isn't in a hurry.

So what can you do for your son when the purpose isn't clear? You pray for him. Ask God to give you wisdom and discernment as his father. Ask God to reveal Himself to your son. Ask God to give him a new heart. Ask God to give your son a love for His Word. Ask God to keep him sexually pure. Ask God to give him a godly wife. Ask God to prepare her for him and bring them together at the right time. Ask God about where he should go to school. Ask God to bring him the right friends. Those are the kinds of things you can be praying about. And one more thing. God loves to answer those kinds of prayers.

Some sons take a longer time than others to find their niche. And even when a man learns his gifts, it is not at all unusual for it to take considerable years before true "congruency" occurs. By "congruency," I speak of that moment in time when a man's gifts and the opportunity for using them most effectively finally come together.[5] Congruency usually doesn't occur until a man has reached midlife, or a place of maturity in which the time is right in God's great tapestry for his life, and he is ready to handle the opportunity. Churchill knew what he was gifted to do, but it was years before the time was right for him to step in as God's man for the hour.

Some sons need help through career counseling to actually find the right pathway for their gifts. There are some excellent tools developed for that very purpose. One such program I can heartily recommend (and it has been very helpful for two of our children) is *Career Direct* from Life Pathways,[6] but there are certainly other excellent such tools. The point is that it is okay if a young man finds himself switching majors in college or trying his hand at more than one thing to see if it is indeed a fit for him.

The Puritan fathers understood this. Let me quote from historian Thomas Hine:

> When early New Englanders spoke of a person's calling, it had
> a far weightier meaning than we give it now. One's occupational call-
> ing—the role you would play in the worldly community—was paral-
> lel to the second and greater calling of becoming one of God's elect...
> The Puritans believed that each person had unique, God-given tal-
> ents. The teenager and his parents would pray and look for interests
> and abilities that suggested the path to their true calling.... False

starts were tolerated, sometimes more than once, when it was clear that the boy had not found a proper calling.[7]

Every son needs a *mission*—a life skill, a trade, a means of making a living, a "calling," as the Puritans affectionately referred to it. To the Puritan, no work was lesser. Every work, whether digging ditches or writing classic works, was considered a "calling." A man's work was his way of honoring God in this life and, in so doing, providing for his family and giving glory to God.

No son wants his father to try to live his life through his son. But every son needs help in wisely discerning his own unique gifts and calling. One of the greatest things you can do for your son is to help him discover a trade or an area of interest that *fits* his skills and his personality.

Don't let him wander through high school and college and expect that he will automatically figure it out. I can't tell you how many young college graduates I have met who are struggling deeply with who they are and where they should be headed in life, and have never received any real guidance or insight from their dads in this most crucial decision of their lives. These young men desperately want to be mentored. They would give anything for wisdom and guidance. It's a shame their fathers didn't do it for them.

HOUSTON, WE HAVE LIFTOFF!

On April 11, 1970, as Jim Lovell, Fred Hayes, and Jack Swaggart of the *Apollo 13* crew strapped themselves into their cockpits for the final lift-off into space, they had no idea what awaited them. They had no idea that they would never walk on the surface of the moon, nor that they would barely ever walk the surface of planet earth again. Yet they had prepared themselves in every conceivable way possible for what was ahead. Those previous endless years of study, those hours of grueling, mind-numbing simulator training, turned out to be the difference between life and death for them. But who could have known?

The point is that a man doesn't know where life will take him. But he can prepare as best he can for the mission that lies before him.

David prepared Solomon. And he prepared him well. When your son is getting ready for liftoff, he'll need some serious preparation. And you can help him just as David helped Solomon.

What did David do to prepare Solomon to step upon the throne? He looked to the assets that Solomon would need if he were going to be effective down the road. And then he did everything he could do to give his son appropriate assistance.

A SON NEEDS A PATH

Life is a very long path. You know what it is to walk down a darkened path. What a difference when someone pulls out a flashlight.

The Word of God is necessary for your son to navigate the path of life. And it's your job to give it to him.

Psalm 119:105 states:

**Your word is lamp to my feet
And a light to my path.**

So to put it another way, it's your job as his father to shine the flashlight of God's Word on the dark path of the future so that your son can find his way.

We have already talked briefly about education. But we didn't talk about *worldview*. Every teacher and every school views the world through a lens. It is the responsibility of a father to make sure that his son is educated through the lens of the Word of God.

David understood the asset of education, and he made sure that Solomon got an education from a biblical worldview. Solomon had a mentor in the godly prophet Nathan, who ministered to his father daily in his courts. It is very likely that Nathan, from time to time, personally instructed the future king in the Scriptures. And it is certain that Solomon observed the wise instruction, counsel, and bold confrontation of sin that Nathan gave to David all the days of his life. Solomon watched Nathan's example of righteous courage and wise counsel right up until the day of his father's death. What an education!

It is also certain that Solomon received training from the best priests and scribes of the land. And from them he learned the book of Deuteronomy. In this book, specifically chapter 17 of this book, God had laid down the laws for the future kings of Israel. In chapter two, we spoke of these—but they are worth repeating because they were so central. Solomon undoubtedly had them memorized as a young prince preparing to take the future throne:

> "He [the king] shall not multiply horses for himself... Neither shall he multiply wives for himself, or else his heart will turn away; nor shall he greatly increase silver and gold for himself." (DEUTERONOMY 17:16–17)

That was the law of God.

The king of Israel was to be different from other kings in the world. He was to depend upon God—not countless horses—to win his battles. He was to remain pure sexually. He was to be generous instead of acquiring overly excessive, corrupting wealth. The world had never known a king like this. What a way to attract attention to the one true and holy God! What a way to lead a nation! What a way to bring glory to God's mighty power in the face of daunting enemies!

This was crystal clear to Solomon. He knew it like the back of his hand.

There was yet one more command from Deuteronomy 17 for the king.

And it was absolutely critical—as in life-and-death.

When a new king took the throne, he was to publicly *write down* a copy of these laws on a scroll in front of the Levitical priest (just to make sure that it was fresh in everybody's mind!). Then he was to *read it all the days of his life* (that's a lot of days), so that he would "fear the Lord his God, by carefully observing all the words of this law" (v.19), and so that he would not "turn aside from the commandment, to the right or to the left" (v. 20).

That's what you call a biblical worldview. The Word of God gets a young man down the path of life. Without it, he's like a blind man with blind guide dog.

INDOCTRINATION OR EDUCATION

In the same way, your son's education is obviously also important. You can't shield your son from a godless worldview. It comes at him every waking moment of his day. And he needs help navigating through the lies of that demonic worldview. It's your job to make sure he is hearing the truth from a balanced, intelligent, fair, and open-eyed biblical perspective—in science, literature, philosophy, etc. The lies of the world are so articulately deceptive that even the best of our young thinkers will be tripped up and deceived without thoughtful, wise, excellent, and thought-provoking teaching. The biblical worldview is the *intelligent* worldview. It tells the truth about life in every field of academia. And he will soon discover this when he gets out there on his own.

I leave it with you and your wife to pray and discern how you might accomplish this goal in his life. In the last chapter we discussed classical schooling and home-schooling. But there are other options as well. Your options are perhaps more wide open than they have ever been in history; there is so much available to you today in terms of a great education from a biblical foundation. For starters, you might pick up Douglas Wilson's excellent little book *Restoring the Lost Tools of Education: An Approach to Distinctively Christian Education*[8] just to get some ideas flowing.

PREPARED WITH POTENTIAL

Before David died, he gave Solomon a final life message. He gave him some advice as he was about to step up to the throne:

> **I am going the way of all the earth. Be strong, therefore, and show yourself a man. Keep the charge of the Lord your God, to walk in His ways, to keep His statutes, His commandments, His ordinances, and His testimonies . . . that you may succeed in all that you do and wherever you turn." (1 KINGS 2:2–3)**

What great advice to leave with your son.

Be a man. Keep the charge. Walk in the ways of the Lord all your days.

Did your dad leave you with such a charge? As Solomon stood by his father's deathbed, these were David's words. Solomon knew he was about to take his father's mantle. These words left an indelible impression upon him. "Do you want to be successful, Solomon? Do you want to be a great king and have great success? Then, my son, be a real man. Do what a real man does. Follow after the Lord always."

When Solomon ascended the throne, he was well prepared for the remaining chapters of his life.

David had done his job. On his deathbed, he knew that he had mentored his son.

Eddie O'Hare faced that storm of gunfire on a Chicago boulevard knowing that he had done the right thing. And by doing the right thing he could face death knowing that he too had mentored his boy.

So how are you coming along with what really matters in life?

Are you preparing your son for what he will one day face when he takes leadership of his own family?

The right thing is rarely the easy thing.

Eddie O'Hare found that out firsthand.

Would he do it all over again?

In a heartbeat.

All healthy men, ancient and modern, Eastern and Western,

know that there is a certain fury in sex that we cannot

afford to inflame, and that a certain mystery and awe must

ever surround it if we are to remain sane.

—G. K. CHESTERTON

CHAPTER EIGHT

SONS AND SEX

(MENTORING THROUGH SEXUAL PURITY)

THERE ARE SHOOTING STARS AND THERE ARE FIXED STARS.

Last night I was down in the pasture checking on my cows. It was a clear evening, and I spent some time looking at Venus, and the formations of fixed stars known as the Big Dipper and the Little Dipper. When I was out there last week, Venus was there and so were the two dippers. They have been there ever since God assigned them to their posts. They will be there tonight and they will be there until there is a new heaven and a new earth. They are fixed stars.

Fixed stars are steady and dependable. When you are lost in a forest or stranded at sea they will help you find your direction. That's what fixed stars do. Some men are fixed stars. They have set their hearts upon a course that is eternal and true. And they have chosen not to depart from it. You can count on them to be there through the most disorienting of storms, or on the darkest and loneliest of nights. They may not be flashy, at least from where we stand. But they are fixed. They are constant. They are steady. They are true.

Last summer we were driving across the Arizona desert headed to California. We had just gotten back on the road after eating a late dinner when suddenly a gigantic meteor streaked across the sky, pierced the horizon, and plunged to the earth. The fireball it created was stunning, enormous—like ten giant fuel tankers colliding in midair. It propelled across the desert night with such force and power that we were absolutely affixed and stunned. Then there was a massive explosion, and as fast as it appeared it was gone. The whole thing happened in a matter of one, maybe two seconds—an unexpected, riveting, breathtaking show. And then sudden darkness. All that was left was a plume of smoke, silently spiraling and rolling, like the final postscripts of a movie, then quietly, unspectacularly fading into the heavens from which it had come.

That is how some men choose to live their lives, like shooting stars. Thomas Watson wrote, "They are called wandering stars because, as Aristotle says, 'They do leap up and down, and wander into several parts of the heaven; and being but dry exhalations, not made of that pure celestial matter as the fixed stars are, they often fall to the earth.'" [1]

Solomon was a shooting star.

He was the brightest, the most brilliant of shooting stars.

When Solomon showed up on the scene, it was not to a few spectators in the desert. The whole world was riveted by his unequalled glory.

Solomon is known as the wisest man who ever lived. In his most spectacular moment, he wrote some of the wisest words ever written. Just sit down sometime and read through the book of Proverbs. Collectively, they are unequalled in their insight and uncanny discernment. Solomon told us where to find wisdom and what we would discover when we found it. Wisdom comes from God alone, he said. Fear God, wrap His wisdom around your heart, discipline your children, love the wife of your youth, choose your friends carefully, remember the power of the tongue, watch out for the death trap of sexual sin. And no one has said it better. Solomon's advice has saved many a man and woman from the path of destruction.

But Solomon was also a fool. You could easily say that he was the most foolish man who ever lived.

He didn't have to be a shooting star.

He could have been a fixed star.

He was given everything that he needed to lead the nation before the Lord. He was given a purpose, a plan, and a path.

That's why Solomon had such potential.

But Solomon got screwed up. And it can all be traced back to women. Multiple women. It was women and sex that got him seriously off course. That's where every man is tempted to go off course. And that includes your son.

As a son, Solomon had great potential. He was one of those guys who lived up to his potential. At least, for awhile.

So King Solomon became greater than all the kings of the earth in riches and in wisdom. (1 Kings 10:23)

That says it all.

Herbert Lockyer describes Solomon's launch into the world:

> Think of the advantages he began with! There were the al-
> most undisputed possession of David's throne, immense stores of
> wealth laid up by his father, exceptional divinely imparted mental
> abilities, the love and high hopes of the people. Solomon's start like

the cloudless dawn of a summer's morning, might have been beautiful all his life through, but it ended in gloom because he wandered
into God-forbidden paths.[2]

No one ever had a better start than Solomon. He was poised to
become a fixed star. But he turned out to be a shooting star that crashed
and burned.

HORSES, MONEY, AND WOMEN

It all started when Solomon decided to violate the commands of Deuteronomy 17. You remember those commands. We've been over them
enough times in this book. First, he gathered horses.... horses and chariots and horsemen—1400 chariots and 12,000 horsemen to be exact. Then
he gathered silver and gold, so much that silver became "as common as
stones in Jerusalem" (1 Kings 10:27). That's a good amount of silver.

But the great downfall of Solomon clearly came when he started to
gather women. You could say that sex was the nail in his coffin.

> **King Solomon loved many foreign women along
> with the daughter of Pharoah... He had seven hundred
> wives, princesses, and three hundred concubines, and his
> wives turned his heart away." (1 KINGS 11:1, 3)**

How did they turn his heart away? They turned his heart away
"after other gods." First Kings 11:5 tells us that "Solomon went after
Ashtoreth... and after Milcom the destestable idol of the Ammonites,"
gods which used sexual perversion and prostitution in their worship.
The Bible goes on to tell us that Solomon, builder of the greatest temple

to God, built altars in the high places to honor these false gods.

> **Then Solomon built a high place for Chemosh the detestable idol of Moab, on the mountain which is east of Jerusalem, and for Molech the detestable idol of the sons of Ammon. (1 KINGS 11:7)**

Do you know about Chemosh and Molech? These were the gods to whom little babies were sacrificed. Can you imagine Solomon tolerating the presence of these false gods in Jerusalem? Can you imagine that Solomon, who had been in the holy presence of almighty God on two occasions, would stoop to personally build an altar to these blood-thirsty, demonic entities? It is unthinkable.

Every Planned Parenthood clinic and every hospital that take the life of children are nothing less than modern altars of Chemosh and Molech. Are there not men today who have covered their own sexual sin through the killing of unborn, unwanted children? We are not so far from Solomon as we may think.

Solomon had the potential to be a fixed star for generations to come. He could have been a great king, and a great father to his sons. But he didn't. And he wasn't.

He crashed and burned in the flames of sexual sin.

He walked into the trap of such addictive and deep sin that he never escaped.

Is it at all possible that you could crash and burn?

We are privileged like Solomon. We are human like Solomon. And, believe me, every man of us can fall like Solomon.

God once warned that if he, Solomon, the writer of the greatest book of wisdom, the book of Proverbs, ever forgot the Giver of that great wisdom to him, God would cause Israel itself to *become a proverb* before the nations of the world (2 Chronicles 7:20).

What a powerful play on words.

Solomon's life became a proverb. It's a proverb we want to avoid. And wise fathers help theirs son to avoid it, as well.

STAYING ON COURSE

Years ago, my son Josh, who was perhaps eight or nine, asked me a question about Solomon.

"Dad, wasn't Solomon the wisest man who ever lived?"

"That's right, Josh. Other than Jesus, he was the wisest man ever," I replied.

"But Dad, didn't he get all messed up?"

"He sure did, Josh. He married seven hundred women and he had three hundred women in addition to his wives."

"So, Dad, how does a man who is so wise get so messed up?"

Good question. Most of us who know the Bible have seriously wondered about that.

After a minute I replied, "Well, Josh, there is a difference between wisdom and obedience. Wisdom is great insight into the truth, but wisdom doesn't guarantee that someone will obey the truth. Solomon knew the truth. He just didn't obey it."

A shooting star is an asteroid that gets off course.

Solomon got off course and like that asteroid he eventually flamed out. His life went up in smoke. Solomon started on course but then he veered off course. So how do you know when you're on course?

- *You're on course when you are in the Word.*
- *You're on course when you walk in humility.*
- *You're on course when you walk in obedience.*

Solomon was smart. He was very smart about life. But he wasn't smart enough to do the most important thing—he didn't obey. Especially when it came to women and sex.

Solomon got it wrong.

We've got to get it right. We can't afford to fool around. Because fooling around with sexual sin has such serious consequences. It causes death to the spiritual soul. Death to a marriage. Heartbreaking death to a family, to our children, and to their children. Sometimes it causes just plain death.

This chapter is about getting it right.

And guys, with His help, we *can* get this one right.

YOUR SON'S GREATEST BATTLE

The single greatest struggle for your son today will be in the area of sexual sin. And that's probably your greatest battle as well.

Let me say it again. Your son will not be able to avoid this struggle for at least two reasons. First, he is a male with a God-given sex drive. Men have always struggled with sexual sin. And second, because of the unprecedented times in which he lives.

Yes, Satan will attempt to use anything to bring your son down as he makes his way in the world: money, ambition, idolatries of every form, including your son's hunger for immediate happiness and gratification.

But get this. It is very important that you get this. Satan has found the Achilles' heel of Western civilization. It's nothing new, of course.

History shows that all great civilizations have seen at their point of final decline a rotting, sexual sin and perversion (Romans 1). In this way, our civilization is nothing new. But I believe we live in unprecedented times, and we are raising our sons in such times and we had better know what we are up against.

I believe (as do my sons) *that God's best and brightest of men are more vulnerable in this area today than ever before in the history of the world.* Why? Let me give you a few reasons.

NO-SHAME OPENNESS

We live in a culture which now embraces as never before with open arms the perversion of homosexuality. And the embrace is open and without shame. The day has come when a man can actually be punished in his career and community standing for daring to express his conscience on this issue, for daring to graciously call homosexuality what God has divinely declared it to be—a perverted and destructive sin that destroys lives and nations (Romans 1:27). Certainly today your son dare not express such an "unkind, insensitive, homophobic" view in a public school setting. He is officially now in the minority. We don't even like the word *sodomy* to be mentioned in our own Christian pulpits and gatherings—even though this is what the Bible explicitly calls it. We are afraid of offending the very people who are dying because of Satan's lies about this sin. We dare not say as did the apostle Paul:

> **Or do you not know that the unrighteous *will not inherit the kingdom of God?* Do not be deceived; neither fornicators, nor idolaters, nor adulterers, nor effeminate, nor homosexuals, nor thieves, nor the covetous, nor drunk-**

ards, nor revilers, nor swindlers, will inherit the king-dom of God." (1 CORINTHIANS 6:9–10, italics mine)

Yet we have so embraced sexual perversion that we are doing something no other culture has done before. Never before in the history of mankind has a major culture attempted to redefine marriage and make homosexual marriage a legitimate "right."[3]

No civilization has ever dared to go this far. Not even Sodom and Gomorrah. This is serious. Of course, it is not limited to homosexuality. Adultery is as commonplace as breathing. Approximately forty years ago, Governor Nelson Rockefeller left his wife and children to marry another woman who was married with four children. The nation was shocked. Never had a public official been so brazen and open about adultery. Yet, several years ago when the Republican mayor of New York City had an affair and divorced his wife, not a ripple of criticism was to be heard. The standards have been seriously lowered.

Single men and women are expected to sleep together before they are married. In fact, if they don't, something must be wrong with them.

Tom Wolfe is a best-selling writer who has been evaluating American culture for close to forty years. He lives in a New York penthouse, hangs out with the upper crust of society, and is not considered a member of the religious side of things. Yet in a recent interview, he gave his evaluation of what has happened to America in regard to sex:

"Yes, there is this puritanism," says Wolfe, "and I suppose we are talking here about what you might call the religious right. But I don't think these people are left or right, they are just religious, and if you are religious, you observe certain strictures on sexual activity—you are against the mainstream, morally speaking. And I do have sympathy with them, yes, though I am not religious. I am simply in awe of it all; the openness of sex. In the 60s they talked about a sexual revolution, but it has become a sexual carnival."[4]

That captures it doesn't it? We are living in a sexual carnival. And it is in this carnival that we are to mentor our sons for godliness.

NO-SHAME ACCESS

We also live in unprecedented times of *accessible* and *in-your-face* sexual temptation. It comes at us from the moment we awaken to the time we lay our heads on our pillows at night. Our sons can't get in a car and drive down the freeway without being assaulted by billboards. They can't turn on the radio or TV, watch a ballgame or an Olympic competition, or walk down the hallway of their high schools where scantily clad girls round every single corner and sit beside them in class. They can't enter a mall or grocery store to buy milk, open a newspaper or magazine. They can't even go to church without being confronted with it openly. Girls just don't get it when they dress in low-cut outfits that reveal most of their breasts and drive guys right up the wall. They have no idea what our sons are dealing with. It's a full frontal satanic assault. It's relentless.

But the greatest assault is through the Internet. Sexual temptation is more accessible, more *invasively and pervasively accessible* than it has ever been before in the history of mankind.

Well, this has been a fun conversation, hasn't it?

Have I encouraged you sufficiently?

We live in a sexual climate that in its extent and intrusion has never been seen before in the history of the world. For that reason, you must help and prepare your son to deal with this insanity. Sons need help now perhaps more than at any other time in history. Your son may have the most godly, disciplined, masculine heart of gold. He may love God with all his heart, mind, and soul. He may be victorious in a hundred ways. But he is excruciatingly vulnerable to being brought down through sexual sin in this supercharged climate of unbridled lust.

You cannot afford *not* to talk with your son about it. And you can't afford not to live out the model he can follow. He needs to be able to talk to you, really talk to you. And he needs to see you living a great model before his eyes.

Your son faces this sexual battle every day of his life, just as you do. My guess is that for him the battle may be even more intense than yours. If he's unmarried (which most guys are nowadays at the peak of their sexual maturity), and since he lives in such times, don't be surprised if his struggle is greater than yours. Understand that. Picture him as a young soldier going into battle. He needs every tool in the box, every training skill, every bit of CIA intelligence. He needs an arsenal equivalent to the U.S. military in fighting this war. Satan is brazenly crafty. He knows that sex is the place, *sex* is where—*if he can get to him early enough* and snatch him before he knows what's hit him—he can bring your son down. So think tactically. Think preemptively.

Preemption is key.

But before you preempt the enemy's attack on your son you are going to have to take some precautions concerning yourself.

That's where we must start. We've said it before and it's worth saying again. If you aren't aggressively fighting sexual sin in your own life, then you can't be any help at all to your son with his battle.

It was Ralph Waldo Emerson who described an acquaintance this way: "The louder he talked of his honor, the faster we counted our spoons." It's the quiet life of obedience that will earn a hearing.

PRONE TO WANDER

Here are the words of Solomon before he began to drift off into sin and get stubborn about it.

> For the LORD gives wisdom; from His mouth come knowledge and understanding. (PROVERBS 2:6)

> My son, let them not vanish from your sight...they will be life to your soul. Then you will walk in your way securely and your foot will not stumble. (PROVERBS 3:21–23)

As we have seen, at the height of his glory, Solomon began to drift away from God. Isolation and coldness seeped into his heart.

How do we know that Solomon grew distant from God? We know by the decisions he made. Solomon began to systematically disobey the commands of God; and his decisions unveiled the true condition of his heart. In fact, he disregarded every command God gave to the kings in Deuteronomy 17.

"If you love me, you will obey me," said Jesus. A man who is close to God genuinely desires to obey Him. When he sins, he feels the pangs of conviction. His heart is grieved over his sin, and he is quick to confess it and try to make things right. But Solomon disobeyed and kept right on disobeying. At any point along the way, he could have repented and been restored. But he did not.

It is entirely possible for a man to appear perfectly fine, to live an outward life of doing all the right things, and yet to be completely isolated from God in his heart. That's how an effective preacher can become suddenly involved in adultery. A man's secret core can look nothing like his outer shell. Solomon kept going to the temple and offering sacrifices. He kept teaching out of the store of his knowledge and wisdom. But in the secrecy of his heart, he became distant from God. And distance led to disobedience. Disobedience that never got purified.

Let me clear something up. By distance from God, I don't mean the *feeling* of distance that comes when we're not experiencing emotional closeness or some spiritual high. These times are part of the normal Christian walk, and every man goes through them. But feelings don't always reflect reality. Feelings come and go. Feelings can never be central. Truth must be central. The truth is that God is right there close to us in those times, even though we don't *feel* that He is close. That's why we have to stay faithful and hang in there for the long haul, like a fixed star. Eventually the fog will lift and we will experience an even greater intimacy with God for having endured through the trial.

The distance that kills us is the distance that *we* create ourselves— by walking away from intimacy with God. Solomon left God. God didn't leave Solomon. How do we walk away from spiritual intimacy? We stop feeding regularly on God's Word. We stop talking with Him as a way of life. We stop allowing Him to probe our hearts and deal with our sin. We pull away from His promptings and we slough off His exhortations through those who love us.

You recall our discussion of the fact that Solomon became a shooting star instead of a fixed star. That is what we want to avoid at all costs.

There are two truths that can save us from becoming shooting stars and getting off course.

First, *it's impossible to be close to God and distant from His Word.*

To have fellowship with God you have to interact with the Bible. When you get into it, you will find that it will get into you.

"Your word I have treasured in my heart, that I may not sin against You," David wrote in Psalm 119:11.

Second, *it's impossible to be close to God and live a life of secret sin.*

God's Word is light. It shines the light in the dark places. It keeps us on our toes when it comes to sin. If Solomon had stayed close to God's Word, if he had kept allowing God's Word to guide him and give him direction, history would have been different. But we know by his disobedience that Solomon quit abiding in God's words. He ignored the command that the king "shall read it *all the days of his life*, that he may learn to fear the Lord his God" (Deuteronomy 17:19, italics mine).

Jesus said: "If you abide in Me, and My words abide in you, ask whatever you wish, and it will be done for you. My Father is glorified by this, that you *bear much fruit, and so prove to be My disciples*" (John 15: 7–8, italics mine). The fruit of Solomon's life proved that he was not abiding in the Word.

If you want to be a great king, you've got to stay in the Word of God. A message on Sunday mornings isn't going to cut it. It didn't cut it for Solomon. You've got to intentionally carve out time to go one-on-one with the Lord, day in and day out. Fifteen minutes is a place to start, just reading Scripture and laying your heart before the Lord. You can build from there. But do what you have to do to stay intimate with the God who loves you and wants to bless you.

It's not always exciting. But it's absolutely essential to your soul.

And can I throw out one other idea that can help you to stay close to the Lord?

Have sex frequently with your wife.

I thought that might get your attention.

And I'm not making this up. It's in the Bible. This is one reason you want to read your Bible. If you don't ever read it, you might get the impression that God is against your having sex with your wife. But he's not.

Solomon was inspired by the Holy Spirit to pen these words in Proverbs:

> **Drink water from your own cistern and fresh water from your own well. Should your springs be dispersed abroad, streams of water in the streets?...Rejoice in the wife of your youth....Let her breasts satisfy you at all times. (PROVERBS 5:15–19)**

Frequent sex with your wife is God's plan. If you don't think that's right, then check out 1 Corinthians 7:1–5. Verse 5 states,

> **Stop depriving one another, except by agreement for a time, so that you may devote yourselves to prayer, and come together again so that Satan will not tempt you because of your lack of self-control.**

Now there's a verse that will motivate you to search the Scriptures.

These two verses are proof that both in the Old and New Testament, God is pleased when you are physically intimate with your wife. And so are you.

If you still don't think it right, then why did God make you with such physical needs? You didn't put those needs in you; God did.

So not only will you need to talk with your son about sex, you may have to talk with your wife about sex. She's not wired the way that you are. You have trouble going three days without sex. Women are wired so that they can go three years. Some have gone three decades and they thought it happened just last week. That's not a put-down; it's just a fact. God did the hardwiring and he decided to do it differently in men and women when it came to sexual needs. Your wife needs to know that you have sexual needs and that they are godly needs.

God made sex. And it is hard for men to be close to the Lord when their sexual needs aren't being met, because they are more prone to give in to sexual temptation. Does that make sense to you? It sure makes sense to me. And there's plenty of sexual temptation out there. Half-naked women are everywhere and so are loose women.

If your godly woman is meeting your sexual needs on a regular basis those other women are not going to have the pull on you that they normally would. But they still have the power to pull you in:

> **The commandment is a lamp, and the teaching is light…to keep you from the evil woman, from the smooth tongue of the adulteress.**
>
> **Do not desire her beauty in your heart, nor let her catch you with her eyelids.**
>
> **For on account of a harlot one is reduced to a loaf of bread, and an adulteress hunts for the precious life. Can a man take fire in his bosom and his clothes not be burned? Or can a man walk on hot coals and his feet not be scorched?**
>
> **So is the one who goes in to his neighbor's wife; whoever touches her will not go unpunished.…When he**

is found, he must repay sevenfold; he must give all of the substance of his house.

The one who commits adultery with a woman is lacking sense; he who would destroy himself does it. (PROVERBS 6:23–32)

If your wife meets your sexual needs, you are not going to be as vulnerable to sexual temptation. When your sexual needs are met, you will not be as tempted when you're on the road or surfing the Net.

In other words, if you've got Rocky Road ice cream in the freezer, there's no reason to go out looking for it late at night at Baskin Robbins.

That's so profound I'm going to move to the next point. And that means three points, actually.

TALKING STRAIGHT

You've got to break the barrier and talk with your son about sex. Your wife can't do that. She's clueless when it comes to understanding what boys are dealing with. Really. She just doesn't get it. That's not her fault. She's not a man. But you are. You understand. He's got to talk to you.

Have you heard about the panda with the gun?

A panda walks into a café. He orders a sandwich, eats it, then draws a gun and fires two shots in the air.

"Why?" asks the confused waiter, as the panda makes toward the exit. The panda produces a badly punctuated wildlife manual and tosses it over his shoulder.

"I'm a panda," he says, at the door. "Look it up."

The waiter turns to the relevant entry and, sure enough, finds an explanation.

"Panda. Large black-and-white bearlike mammal, native to China. Eats, shoots, and leaves."[5]

That story is from a best-selling book that emphasizes the importance of punctuation. If punctuation is ignored, the meaning can be distorted.

When you talk with your son, you want to be clear.

So let me put on the table three real basic principles that will help you overcome the fear of talking to your son about sex so that you can make things real clear:

1. Talk to him early and wisely.

When I say early, I mean begin the conversations when he is six or seven. Catch him before somebody else does. And these days, it's much earlier than when you and I were kids. Now I'm in a bind here. A time-page bind. But I have written an entire chapter about how to do this in *Point Man* (chapter ten).[6] Beg, borrow, or steal the book if you need to, because it will coach you word by word, step by step how to talk to your son about sex, and especially earlier on. You're obviously not going to tell him what you would tell a twelve-year-old. He can only handle so much emotionally. So how much can he handle? Ask God to give you the wisdom to discern that. You want some good news? God will answer that prayer.

Just don't wait until he's twelve to start talking straight about sex with him. Someone will have already gotten to him by then.... trust me. So, yes, you need to be wise in what you disclose. But fear not. God will guide your conversations. You will be shocked at how he will guide your conversations.

2. Talk to him honestly.

Here's the second thing you can do. Read through the book of Proverbs with your son. Just take a paragraph and read through it. And then let the Lord take it from there. Proverbs talks about a lot of issues that a son will face in life. And it is specifically written from a father to his son to give his son wisdom for all the issues he will face as he walks down the trail of life.

One of those issues is sex. And Proverbs comes back to that issue time and time again. If Proverbs is the specific book that contains the wisdom a father needs to give to his son, then why not take advantage of it? And as you do this you will get into all kinds of great discussions on sex. And then the questions will start flying.

"So, Dad, what about masturbation?"

Now there's a question that can bring on a heart attack.

You see, most guys don't want their sons to ever ask them about masturbation because they don't know what to say. I think you do know what you ought to say. You just don't want to say it because you don't want to tell him about your struggles in that area. But he needs to know that you struggled. And he needs for you to talk to him about it. That will help him tremendously.

Talk to him about his thought life and the fact that masturbation is an issue of self-control that really is mental. Sure it's a physical release, but if he can't learn to control the need for physical release before he's married, how will he ever deal with it after he's married?

Masturbation is an opportunity for a son to learn sexual self-control. He can fight to control it or it will control him. Does your son know this? No. Do you know it? Yes. So talk to him about it.

Here's a good way to have a discussion about masturbation. Bring it up before he does. Bring it up before it ever enters his mind. Bring it up before his body begins to change.

Tell him what it is.

*And then tell him to **never** start doing it.* Warn him off like you warn off a train in the middle of the night when the bridge up ahead has washed out.

Masturbation is a major issue. For some guys it becomes like alcohol or cocaine. It takes over their lives. I know alcoholics who wish they had never taken that first drink.

I know some men who are successful in business, committed to the Lord, and devoted to their wives, who have hired prostitutes so they can masturbate in their presence. These men are wracked with guilt, and they are taking radical steps to kill this sin. But they will tell you that masturbation was the addiction that dominated their life. If you find yourself in that kind of addictive situation, you need to make your way to www.netaccountability.com and check out this ministry. These guys are friends of mine and they are able to help guys who think there is no hope. There is hope. You just need some guys to help you get out of the pit and stay out.

Does masturbation become that strong in every man's life to that degree? No, but it certainly has the potential. So why not get to your son early and *warn him off from ever beginning in the first place?* You may be thinking that it's not possible. It is possible. But it takes the mentoring of a clued-in father to happen.

AN UNFORGETTABLE INTERVIEW

I have been privy to a couple of very frank conversations with a small group of godly young men from a Christian university campus. These guys were being open and honest about their sexual struggles. I'm going to reconstruct some of the highlights from that interaction. A lot of questions were put on the table. They gave some remarkable and insightful answers. I'll warn up front. This conversation is not for the faint of heart. It went sort of like this:

Q: How many Christian guys you know would say that they struggle with masturbation?

A: 99.9 percent of the guys we know admit to having struggled with it. The common consensus is that the other .1 percent is lying.

Q: Have you ever talked to your dad about masturbation?

A: With one exception, no.

Q: The world says masturbation is a natural, normal, healthy outlet. How do you respond to that?

A: Masturbation is destructive. It causes a guy to think about sex as only that, sex—pure, unadulterated, self-fulfilling sex. It begins privately, but it is the *gateway to all other sexual sin*. What happens is that a guy starts with masturbation. He experiences a physical high. But soon, that isn't enough. So he starts looking at pornography while masturbating to get his high. Then that's not enough. So he just starts actually having sex with real women. With some guys, prostitution can get into the picture. And then there are the guys who still want to go further.... so they get into homosexuality purely out of looking for the next high.

Q: How do you think premarital masturbation hurts a future marriage?

A: Well, we're not married yet. But we know guys who are. And what we hear from them makes sense to us. For one thing, a guy who habitually masturbates can get so good at satisfying himself that he may find that his wife isn't able to at least initially give him that same sensational high. That puts their sex on a performance basis (even if unspoken).

But the worst damage is that a habit of masturbating has produced a mind-set, a focus on sexual self-fulfillment. In marriage, intercourse is about fulfilling the other person's needs and having the surpassing experience of mutual satisfaction. The world can't even come close in that department. But for this to happen in marriage, a guy has to be sacrificial, patient, looking for ways to meet his wife's needs. (And vice versa.) It's all about Ephesians 5, loving your wife as Christ loves the church. And, of course, that kind of sex is so much better than the world's self-satisfying sex. Intercourse the way God designed it is so far superior that the Bible even uses marriage as an illustration of the beauty and mystery of His relationship with the church, His bride.

Q: How does a guy get off the masturbation track?

A: Well, it's all in the mind. It's inside the heart. So there's got to be a starvation of the bad stuff in our minds, and feeding of the good stuff (i.e., Scripture) in our minds. But it's more than that. Because at some point, a guy has got to come to a place where he just hates it. The thought of sexual sin has to make him feel disgusted, like throwing up. That's the goal.

The biggest thing that has helped us guys has been HOPE.

Really, a guy just needs to know that somebody else has defeated it. To discover that "my dad doesn't do this," or "this guy over here hasn't done it for a year." or "this guy over here hasn't done it for four years" — that's unbelievably encouraging.

Q: If there was one thing you would say to your sons someday about masturbation, what would it be?

A: I would tell my son, never start. Never do it even once.

These young men have a lot of wisdom. They have learned some things the hard way. And they are looking forward to a great future when they get married because they are committed to living God's way.

3. Talk to him often.

Talking to your son once about sex—having the "sex talk," as they used to call it—isn't going to be enough. That's like a guy telling his wife once on their wedding day that he loves her, and then not being able to figure out why he ever needs to say it again. Ask your son, "How's it going?" Bring it up in natural situations. If he confesses to failure in this area, treasure that confession and give him hope. Every man is human. Every man sins sexually, even if only in his mind.

Talk about the stuff that's happening in the culture that violates God's Word, and how they can think about it and confront it. Just keep on talking as life goes by.

Did Solomon struggle with masturbation? We don't know. But it would be no shocker. The thing is that, of course, with one thousand women at his disposal, he had progressed far beyond masturbation.

Do you want to defeat sexual sin? Do you want to see your son win the battle against sexual temptation? Do you desire that he be a virgin when he is married? So does God. Then tell him this. Express this strongly to him, that nothing would be more blessed to him and to his future wife. And pray for him. For he will be a rare treasure. And he needs your prayer for him in the battle.

Solomon decided he loved sin too much to fight it. Don't let that happen to you. And don't let it happen to your son.

When a man gets disoriented and lost in a remote wilderness, he only needs one thing to find his way out. And I don't mean a compass. If a man is lost in the wilderness without a compass, he can still find his way. All he needs is a clear sky so that he can locate the North Star.

The North Star isn't flashy and it doesn't shoot across the sky. It stays put and does its job. The North Star is a fixed star. And that's your responsibility to your son before God. If you do nothing else for him, stay committed to Christ and to your wife. By so doing, you will help your son find his way in a world that is utterly lost and without direction.

The parent's life is the child's copybook.

—JOHN PARTRIDGE

CHAPTER NINE

THE KRAMER OF JUDAH

(MENTORING THROUGH MANLY COMMUNICATION, PART 1)

SOLOMON HAD A SON BY THE NAME OF REHOBOAM.

He should have named him Kramer.

Or Seinfeld. Or even George.

You see, like the characters on Seinfeld, Rehoboam never grew up. At forty-one (1 Kings 14:21), he was still acting like he was in high school. Rehoboam was a perpetual adolescent. And forty-one-year-old men who are trying to stay young and hip make lousy kings.

When Rehoboam should have been in the prime of his life and wisdom, he was nothing but an overgrown junior high kid. Rehoboam was forty-one years of age but he wasn't a man. Rehoboam was a perpetual adolescent. Picture a forty-one-year-old man with an earring, a ponytail, and a deep concern over the condition of his abs. That's Rehoboam, the perpetual life of the party.

Perpetual adolescence is the curse of modern American culture. Everyone wants to be young instead of mature. That's a recipe for disaster. Joseph Epstein, in his insightful essay *The Perpetual Adolescent*, has noted that life has historically been viewed as having a beginning, a middle, and an end:

> Each part, it was understood, had its own advantages and detractions, but the middle—adulthood—was the lengthiest and most earnest part, where everything serious happened and much was at stake. To violate any of the three divisions of life was to go against what was natural and thereby to appear unseemly, to put one's world somehow out of joint, to be, let us face it, a touch, and perhaps more than a touch grotesque.
>
> Today, of course, it has all been shattered. The ideal almost everywhere is to seem young for as long as possible.... Youth is no longer viewed as a transitory state which one passes on the way from childhood to adulthood, but an aspiration, a vaunted condition in which, if one can only arrange it, to settle in perpetuity.[1]

Or to put it another way, the goal is to be young forever.

That's a lousy goal for a man or woman to pursue. Chasing youth is a race in the wrong direction. The goal is not to stay young; the goal is maturity. In writing to young Timothy, Paul said, "We proclaim Him, admonishing every man and teaching every man with all wisdom, so that we may present every man complete in Christ" (Colossians 1:28). Paul didn't want believers to worry about their abs or thinning hair—he wanted them to grow up in Christ.

Rehoboam never grew up. He was like a green banana that kept attempting to stay green. The goal of a green banana is to look in the mirror one day soon and see yellow. For a banana, yellow is maturity.

Yellow for a banana represents wisdom, discernment, and maturity. If Rehoboam had been a banana, he would have been yellow about turning yellow. Becoming mature was just too stressful. It was a lot easier just to hang out with his buddies from college and not commit to anything of importance.

Rehoboam was sort of an Old Testament Kramer. At an age when Jerry, Elaine, George, and Kramer should have been married and raising children, they are still hanging out in the coffee shop trying to figure out what movie they want to go to that night. As Epstein observes about shows like *Seinfeld* and *Friends,* "Growth and development aren't part of the deal. They are still, somehow, in spirit, locked in a high school of the mind, eating dry cereal, watching a vast quantity of television, hoping to make ecstatic sexual scores."[2] That's the way life is when you're nineteen these days—and it's increasingly more the way life is when you're forty. But it's not much of a life.

> The old hunger for life, the eagerness to get into the fray, has been replaced by an odd patience that often looks like passivity. In the 1950s, people commonly married in their twenties, which may or may not have been a good thing, but marriage did prove a forcing house into adulthood, for men and women, especially where children issued from the marriage, which they usually did fairly quickly.... By 30, one was supposed to be settled in life: wife, children, house and job. Today most people feel they can wait to get serious about life. Until then one is feeling one's way, still deciding, shopping around, contributing to the formation of a new psychological type: the passive-nonaggressive.[3]

The new passive-nonaggressive. That encapsulates the culture of reluctant adulthood in America today. It was W. H. Auden who wrote, "Obviously it is normal to think of oneself as younger than one is, but it is fatal to want to be younger."[4]

When it came time for Rehoboam to assume his father's throne, he flat-out wasn't ready. He could handle sitting on the throne, wearing the crown, and sipping wine. He just couldn't rule with any kind of sense.

There were two things that held Rehoboam back from emerging from adolescence and becoming a wise and mature leader.

The first was a bad example.

The second was bad friends.

A BAD EXAMPLE

I have observed something. When dads don't have a healthy mentoring relationship with their sons, those sons instinctively pick up on their father's weakest traits. And it is not uncommon that they will emulate them as adults, even taking them further than their fathers. That's what happened to Rehoboam. Rehoboam followed his father's worst examples in leadership.

• *Solomon was sexually immoral. Rehoboam followed suit.* In his brief and uninspiring reign, he managed to acquire eighteen wives and sixty concubines, and to father twenty-eight sons and sixty daughters (2 Chronicles 11:21). He gave his sons foreign wives the way most fathers give their sons baseball cards (2 Chronicles 11:23). Like father, like son.

• *Solomon abandoned the law of God. So did Rehoboam.* We are told that "he and all Israel with him forsook the law of the Lord" (2 Chronicles 12:1), and that "he did evil because he did not set his heart to seek the

Lord" (2 Chronicles 12:14). Like father, like son.

• *Solomon was a harsh leader.* Now, we haven't discussed this weakness of Solomon's. But at a certain point in his reign, Solomon became a harsh ruler. He began by levying forced labor among the people (1 Kings 5:13–18; 9:15). Then in his obsessive quest to build and build, Solomon became a harsh taskmaster. He took the young men of the northern tribes and drafted them into his army of construction crews. Solomon was focusing on turning Jerusalem into the crown jewel city of the world. But Jerusalem was in the south and he was using the young men of the north to get the work done. Not only did Solomon treat them like slaves, but also they were far removed from their families and friends. Solomon's harshness with the northern tribes was like salt in a wound.

ROT OR RIOT

The end result was rebellion. That's what harsh leadership does. It leads to rebellion—in some way, shape, or form. The rebellion may come in the form of a *passiveness* that absolutely drives the already driven father crazy. It may come in the form of a *secret rebellion*—on the Internet or outside of the house, somewhere in a dark corner of indulgence. Believe me, the possibilities are endless. And the father will have no clue, at least not until the rebellion is well down the path. (This is what happened to Solomon.) Or the rebellion can be an *overt*, in-your-face, "I don't care what you think or what this does to you" kind of rebellion. (This is eventually what happened under Rehoboam.)

Rebellion against harshness doesn't start out as rebellion. Children don't usually just rebel against a harsh parent overnight. They usually try to connect first. Why? Because in their heart of hearts they want to connect. They may not do it very well, but that's to be expected. They're kids. Many sons won't verbally express their feelings, but the signs of hurt and frustration and distance are there for all to see. If a dad doesn't pick up on it, he can lose his son.

The day will come under harsh leadership that a son will lose respect and give up. In his mind he will conclude: "He doesn't understand me. He isn't really listening. I'll never ever really win his true approval. He's wrapped up in his own troubles, his own world, his own agenda, and that's the only thing that really matters to him." So what does he do? He goes out and finds someone who does understand him.... some kid or group of kids that are just as confused as he is and are searching for dignity and connection just like he is.

That's what happened with Rehoboam. And that's what happened with the kingdom of Israel. The harsh rule of Solomon crushed the spirits of the people and led to rebellion. His elders and counselors certainly saw the problem (2 Chronicles 10:6–7). But Solomon was on a mission and hearing none of it. To Solomon's surprise, the rebellion in Israel was led by one of Solomon's most trusted leaders, Jeroboam (1 Kings 11: 28), a worthy man from whom he would have least expected it. And that is often how it happens. It was Thomas Adams who observed, "To rot and to riot differ by one small letter." Under a harsh leader, you can count on two things. The people will rot and eventually they will riot. That happens in nations and it happens in families.

Joseph Stalin was a harsh leader and a mass murderer. They are still adding up the numbers of those who were murdered in Russia under his harsh regime. Stalin bragged to Winston Churchill that "tens of millions of Russian peasants had been dealt with."

In 1941, a group of British officials was visiting Stalin, and one had the gall to ask him how long the killing of his own people would continue. Stalin replied, "As long as it is necessary."

Is it any wonder that Stalin's wife committed suicide and his oldest son made the attempt to do so? Harshness kills people. Sometimes it kills physically and sometimes it kills them emotionally.

Solomon became harsh when he abandoned biblical authority. Instead of leading out of kindness and firmness, he became harsh. And he passed on this poor example to his son.

Solomon was harsh. Rehoboam became even harsher than his father. Solomon did mentor his son. He just mentored him in the wrong things.

Every father mentors his sons. But most of them are oblivious to it.

BAD FRIENDS

The second thing that kept Rehoboam from becoming a wise leader was his terrible selection of friends. Rehoboam underestimated the rotting effect of bad friends. He thought he could hang around these guys, have a few laughs, and remain unaffected. But instead his friends ended up pulling him down. Their advice caused him to lose 10/12ths of the kingdom that his father and grandfather had built. And he lost it in three days.

Never underestimate the importance of friends in your life.... or your son's life. One bad friend can undo in a very short time what a father may have spent years building into his son's life. It only takes one. That's why we are going to spend an entire chapter looking at this issue. Thomas Fuller was right: "Better fare hard with good men than feast it with bad."

A man can't grow out of adolescence into healthy manhood when he is following his dad's bad example and when he's got a bunch of bad apples as friends. That's a recipe for disaster.

REHOBOAM'S SHORT STORY

Let me give you the CliffNotes version of what happened to Rehoboam. (You can read the full story in 1 Kings 12 and 2 Chronicles 9–10.)

Solomon died leaving the throne to Rehoboam. But there was trouble in Jerusalem. From day one, the kingdom was teetering on collapse. A very popular rebel named Jeroboam came before the new king with "all of Israel" (2 Chronicles 10:3) with a request. Who was this Jeroboam?

Jeroboam had been a highly regarded leader under Solomon. He had assisted Solomon in huge building projects. But he had also been the chosen representative of the northern tribes regarding their complaints to Solomon. Finally God had sent a prophet to Jeroboam telling him that because of Solomon's sin, ten of the twelve tribes would be torn away from the kingdom, and he, Jeroboam, would be made king over them. When Solomon got wind of this, he went after Jeroboam with a vengeance and tried to kill him. But Jeroboam escaped to Egypt.

On the day of Solomon's death, the people asked Jeroboam to return home. But Jeroboam did a surprising thing. Instead of leading a rebellion, he went before the fledgling king with one request on behalf of the people: "Please lighten the heavy yoke of hard service of your father, and we will serve you." It was a reasonable request. They weren't asking for the world. The people of Israel simply wanted a fair approach to the labor that would inevitably be asked of them by their new king.

Rehoboam sent the people away and told them he would have an answer for them in three days. Then he consulted with two groups of advisors. The first group were the elders who had served his father, Solomon. They said, "If you will be kind to this people and please them and speak good words to them, they will be your servants forever." This was wise, biblical advice. And it came from mature men with years of experience.

The second group Rehoboam checked in with were his buddies from college. "Are you kidding?" they said. "You need to put the fear of Rehoboam in them! Tell them, 'My little finger is thicker than my father's sexual organ.'" (Yes, that is literally what they said.) They went on, "Tell them, 'You haven't seen anything yet! My dad disciplined you with whips, but I will discipline you with scorpions.'" Well, that was real wise thinking. Tell these people you are going to make their lives absolutely miserable. That should win their allegiance.

Take one guess as to whose advice Rehoboam took. You guessed it. He listened to his drinking buds that wouldn't have recognized wisdom if it ran over them in a truck.

When the people came back three days later, Rehoboam "answered them harshly" (2 Chronicles 10:13), just as his young advisors had suggested. "So then, the king did not listen to the people" (v. 15).

The people of the ten northern tribes had been rotting. Now they were going to riot by breaking away from Rehoboam, establishing a new nation, and bowing before Jeroboam as king.

THE PRICE OF TALKING WITHOUT LISTENING

It's a serious error to not listen to the people in your kingdom. For us, that means our wives and kids. *Listen* is the key word here. Children need to be able to express their feelings. They need to be heard out. Your home needs to be a place of refuge, not attack. It needs to be a place where they know they will be listened to and understood. Listening is not a weakness. It is a huge strength. And it is very wise.

Listening means being quiet as your people speak. You can't listen and lecture at the same time. And listening is not about winning. You are not listening to get the advantage so that you can have the "slam-dunk" comeback. Listening implies that there are other viewpoints besides yours. And those viewpoints are valuable. Listening is about giving dignity to your children, validating their concerns, and granting them understanding, just as your heavenly Father understands you.

This is probably going to come as a shock to you, but even in my "wise and aged years," I am not always right. I know that's hard to believe. Actually, it's very easy to believe. I hate to admit it, but it's true. And my children need to know that they can approach me as a man who knows he isn't always right and is willing to see it and admit it.

Rehoboam's story is short because he didn't listen. No sooner had he issued his decision than the ten northern tribes walked away and set up their own kingdom—the nation of Israel, with Jeroboam as their king. And they never returned. Second Chronicles 10:19 put it this way: "And Israel has been in rebellion against the house of David to this day."

What a sad story.

TEN LOST TRIBES

It's a sad story for two reasons. The ten tribes were lost to Judah. They would become the nation of Israel, the northern kingdom. Jeroboam, the new king of the ten tribes, had a great opportunity to do it God's way. But he didn't. Jeroboam immediately went about setting up a counterfeit religion in an attempt to win the loyalty of the people.

Jeroboam set up a new power center, a new temple, with new priests and two golden calves, saying: "Behold, your gods, O Israel, that brought you up from the land of Egypt" (1 Kings 12:28). His counterfeit religion with its counterfeit priests and two counterfeit temples poisoned the well of the new nation. It was downhill from there. There was never a good or godly king to follow Jeroboam on the throne of Israel. The ensuing murders and power grabs, the evils of every king without exception, the perverse worship of idols and killing of the prophets of God—all of this eventually led to God's judgment and the erasing of those tribes from the face of the earth. That is sad to the extreme. Today no one knows where the ten tribes are. They were carried into captivity and never heard from again.

Not many men can manage to destroy nearly eighty years of work in three days—yet that is precisely what Rehoboam managed to do. His grandfather, David, had united the twelve tribes and served them as king for forty years. His son, Solomon, also reigned over the nation for forty years. Rehoboam's reign over the twelve tribes of Israel lasted three days.

Rehoboam could have made a wise decision and united the country with this one decision. It was a golden opportunity to win the hearts of the ten northern tribes and strengthen the entire nation.

But Rehoboam didn't have the maturity to lead out of grace and flexibility. He just had to be a hard guy. He was like some twelve-year-old on a playground trying to be tough. Only by God's grace did he end up with the remaining two tribes, which became the nation of Judah. God didn't keep these tribes for Rehoboam. He kept them so that he could fulfill his promise to David—his promise of an heir who would one day rule on the throne forever. God kept the throne of David over Judah so that the Messiah could be born. You could say Rehoboam was one fortunate guy to be the beneficiary of his grandfather's faith.

But his grandfather couldn't save him from becoming a fool. David did everything he could to mentor Solomon. I'm sure that he expected Solomon to then mentor his sons. But Solomon, the wisest man on the earth, did not have enough smarts to mentor his own son. And so it happened that the wisest man in the land raised a son who was one of the greatest fools in all of history.

Here's a tip.

Knock off the harsh stuff.

It doesn't work.

You don't have to be the wisest man on earth to figure that out.

There is little we touch, but we leave

the print of our fingers behind.

—RICHARD BAXTER

CHAPTER TEN

HOW TO CRUSH YOUR SON SO HE WILL NEVER RECOVER

(MENTORING THROUGH MANLY COMMUNICATION, PART 2)

THE JOB OF A FATHER CAN BE REDUCED DOWN TO TWO WORDS: construct and crush. Much of what a father is called to do is nothing less than hands-on construction. Good fathers work hard at building their faith, building their marriages, and building their children to become mature and responsible adults. That's construction. And good fathers also build fences and tree houses and forts in the bedroom out of pillows, blankets, and extra chairs. That's construction.

Fathers are also called to crush. When the ice maker goes out in the refrigerator and you've got family coming over for Thanksgiving, everyone looks to Dad to be a crusher. So you run out to the store and get a couple of bags of ice, you bring it home and then what do you do? You crush it. You either get out a hammer and give the bag a few whacks or you just drop the bag outside on the patio. Good fathers are very creative at crushing ice.

Fathers are also called to crush spiders, cockroaches, beetles, and scorpions that make their way into the family compound. Fathers also crush trash deeper into the can and they crush cans with their hands just to impress their kids. Fathers are called by the Lord to enter into a ministry of crushing.

But they never crush their sons.

AUTHORITY VERSUS AUTHORITARIANISM

When fathers use authority they construct. When they become authoritarian they crush people.

Rehoboam was an "authoritarian." He had to be a hard guy with the ten northern tribes and as a result he lost them. He had to be harsh and tough when it wasn't necessary. And he blew up the entire nation by doing so.

Another word for harsh leadership is authoritarian leadership. There's a big difference between *leading with authority* and *being an authoritarian*. Sons need authority. But they are crushed under authoritarianism. Authority is biblical. Authoritarianism is anti-biblical. Let me contrast the two for you, and as I do, you will probably see yourself in some cases on the side of authoritarianism. I'm not saying that's okay, but I am saying that it's normal, for it is human nature to tend toward authoritarianism instead of authority. And when you see these traits in yourself and are saddened by them, all the better. That's when you can make some needed corrections. I've had to make those corrections over the years and so have you. We will undoubtedly need to make more in the future. We can never stop working on these corrections.

If you don't make the corrections away from authoritarianism you will at some point crush your son's inner soul and affect him for life. I know you don't want to do that. You wouldn't be reading this book if you wanted to do that.

So what are the differences between authority and authoritarianism?

- *Authority* is kind. *Authoritarianism* is dismissive and rude.
- *Authority* is firm, looking into the heart of the child. *Authoritarianism* is overly concerned with the letter of the law, often completely overlooking the heart of the child.
- *Authority* disciplines. *Authoritarianism* abuses—through manipulation, or power pulls, or verbal undressing, or worse.
- *Authority* is open and approachable. *Authoritarianism* is easily threatened, and therefore discourages being approached.
- *Authority* is thoughtful and intentional. *Authoritarianism* is explosive.
- *Authority* is consistent. *Authoritarianism* is unpredictable and can jump out and bite off a head at any given moment.
- *Authority* encourages people and builds them up. *Authoritarianism* discourages people by focusing on their faults.
- *Authority* holds out an open hand of generosity. *Authoritarianism* is stingy—stingy with praise, stingy with kind acts, stingy with money—clutching its hand in a tight fist.

These next three are very important and I hope you will grab onto them.

- *Authority* provides structure in which lines are clear, problems are faced, consequences are fair and swift, and conflict is resolved. (In other words, authority is characterized by healthy conflict resolution.) *Authoritarianism* promotes an environment of tyranny that crushes the spirit and leaves conflict unresolved. Unresolved conflict is almost the byword for authoritarianism.

- A house led by authority is *not child centered*. It is *God centered* and *parent/principle driven*. A house ruled by authoritarianism oddly enough tends to become child centered. That's because authoritarianism is *reactive*, rather than proactive. And it is usually driven by an underlying anxiety, fear, depression, or anger.
- A man who leads with *authority* thinks a lot about the personalities and needs of his people. A man who leads out of *authoritarianism* is concerned primarily with one personality and need—his.

In the end, authority promotes connection, while authoritarianism kills connection. And authority unites families, while authoritarianism splits them apart.

HARSH = ANGRY

Do you know how wives and kids think of a dad who is authoritarian? They think of him as an angry and unhappy man. *Angry* is the key word here. Your son sees you as an angry and unhappy man. If you were such a son, would you want to grow up to be like your dad?

I run across men all the time who aren't splitting nations, but they are destroying their families. I have seen men who would never commit adultery or divorce their wives, but they are destroying their families by being harsh and authoritarian. They make a decision and by golly that's it! An authoritarian husband or father is a man who demands unquestioned obedience to his authority. He rules with an iron hand. There is no grace and there is no mercy. It's his way or the highway. There is *never* any flex or give, even if he knows he made the wrong decision.

In Colossians 3:21, the apostle Paul pens a message from the King of Kings to fathers: "Fathers, do not exasperate your children, so that they will not lose heart." I was impressed with the comments on this verse of a wonderful scholar of New Testament Greek, T. K. Abbott:

> A child frequently irritated by over-severity or injustice, to which, nevertheless, it must submit, acquires a spirit of sullen resignation, leading to despair.[1]

Abbott knows his Greek, but he also knows the damage that harsh fathers can inflict on their families. He uses the term *over-severity*. That describes the essence of the harsh man. Now don't misunderstand. Fathers need to be firm in their discipline. If you draw a line, your children need to know that you will not back off from the principle. But it is possible to become a virtual tyrant in your home and come to love the "lines" more than you love your family. If you make a decision and it happens to be the wrong one, then be man enough to change it and say you were wrong! That spirit of openness to the Lord will keep you from getting harsh and authoritarian.

REMORSE WITHOUT CHANGE

With a harsh man, there is little affection or sensitivity to the emotional well-being of his wife or children. If his heart is severely hardened, then when he has damaged them by his harshness he doesn't let up and he doesn't apologize. If his heart is not totally hardened, he ends up feeling remorse. But his remorse is ineffectual, and here is why. His remorse is always with qualifications, explanations, partial blame placed somewhere else. Then a day or two later, there he is again, back to his old harsh self. His remorse has been meaningless, serving to only deepen a son's disrespect and drive his family further and further away from him.

Trust me. This is not how you want to live.

And by the way, didn't we cover this stuff in the last chapter? Well, we opened the discussion in the last chapter. But authoritarianism is such a problem with Christian men that it deserves more than just a passing discussion. So consider this a two-by-four right in the chops. I need it and so do you.

An authoritarian dad creates a suffocating environment in his home. There is little joy, humor, or laughter. But there is criticism galore. The atmosphere he creates—like the ambience of a trashy, smoke-filled restaurant—chokes the life out of his wife and kids. As soon as they get the chance, it's no surprise when one or more of them bolt. They just can't take the negativity, criticism, and complaining.

Perhaps you heard about the monks in a remote mountain monastery who had taken a vow of silence. They could only speak once every ten years and they were allowed only two words.

At the end of his first ten years, a monk gets his opportunity to speak.

He goes into the office of the head monk, looks him in the eye, and says, "Food bad."

Ten years later he gets another shot. He walks into the office and says, "Bed hard."

A decade goes by and again he visits the office of the chief monk.

"I quit," says the monk.

"I'm not surprised," says the head monk in return. "You've been complaining since the day you got here."

I threw in that bad joke to try and lighten things up a little bit. It is a very sad discussion when the subject is fathers who are critical and complaining. That kind of negativity ruins sons, daughters, wives, and cocker spaniels. No one can live in such a stifling environment of negativity.

A son grows up in a home where Scripture is taught. He goes to church every Sunday with his family. Maybe he goes to one of the best Christian schools and gets a biblical worldview. He does all the right things, jumps through all the hoops—straight A's, good athlete, leader. He uses all the right Christian lingo and never bucks the system. Then one day, he walks away from God and never looks back.

How could this happen?

What you have to understand here is that this son is not simply walking away from God. He's walking away from his father. For the first few decades of your son's life, you are the primary picture of who God is and what God is like. His comprehension of his heavenly Father begins with you. It doesn't matter what they tell him in church or at school. You are his God-figure. He knows you are not perfect, but he's constantly making that unconscious connection. Dad is unapproachable. (God must be unapproachable.) Dad is distant. (God must be distant.) Dad is always on my case; I can never please him. It's all about my performance. (God accepts me on the basis of my performance too.) Dad is never to be questioned. (There is no room for questions with God.) Dad is always upset and angry. (God must be an angry God.) Dad is unkind. (God is not a kind God.) If a dad is emotionally unempathethic and authoritarian, then God must also be this way.

Do you see the tragedy? Here is a father who would probably give his life for his son, yet this very son walks away from him and from the God he loves. You see, at some point, this son is no longer in the safe cocoon of his home. He hits hard things in life as every young man does. At the very point in his life when he needs to know Yahweh, the God of provision and faithfulness and grace and understanding, what is he hearing in his mind?

Guilt tapes are playing over and over in his mind, especially if he is a tenderhearted soul who cares deeply about things like honesty and integrity. And in his mind, there is no grace. His spirit is crushed. And so in order to survive, he walks away.

Let me repeat this. *In order to survive, he walks away.* Just like Israel walked away from Rehoboam.

TEACHING YOUR SON TO MASTER ANGER

This chapter was supposed to be a chapter on mentoring your son in mastering anger. But can you now see that the only way to do this is by mastering anger in your own life? Sons who grow up with dads who discipline their tongues, who act out of grace and mercy, who are not driven by anger—these sons don't struggle with deep-set anger in their own lives. Deep-seated anger in the son is too often rooted in an inner rage and anger toward his father.

BLIND MEN

Even as I write this, I am very aware of something. A man who has developed such a habitual need for control is the last to see it and admit to it. He has made himself blind. In fact, all is justified in his eyes. Harsh men are almost always defensive. And this is where they hang themselves. If a man is defensive, he can't listen to good counsel—from his wife, from his children, from anybody else who is looking out for his welfare. Some guys are flat-out threatened by any input that would correct any attitude or behavior in their lives.

If a man is crushing his children, he is also crushing his wife. And that is really bad news. The great value of his wife's partnership is being completely missed; and if she loves him, he has become the source of constant pain and unhappiness to her. He's become like Henry Higgins in *My Fair Lady* shouting, "Why can't a woman be like a man?! Why can't she be more like . . . me?!!" This is also bad news for his daughters. They are learning that it's all about performance, and a huge emotional hole develops in their hearts . . . a hunger to be loved and cherished unconditionally. Girls like this walk around looking for ways to fill that hole. And we know the tragic results of that.

It's also bad news for his sons. His sons are learning from him how to disrespect women, how to excuse their own sin and blame others, how to control through manipulation and anger. They are learning that respect is something you don't have to earn. You simply demand it. They are learning that women are to be managed and subjugated—or to put it bluntly, they are to be used. It's not a pretty picture. These sons are being set up for serious problems with women when they become men.

If you are one of these hard guys who crush your family, then let me give you some more bad news. Do you know that if you don't live with your wife in an understanding way, God won't answer your prayers (1 Peter 3:7)? God doesn't respond to a man who thinks he's a god in his own home.

There are all kinds of reasons that a man becomes harsh. I'm not a psychologist—I could probably use a psychologist. But I've picked up a few things in my time of working with men over the last twenty-five years.

Maybe you had a harsh parent: Your mother was harsh and controlling (while your father was passive), or your dad was harsh and controlling. So because you were disrespected in all your years growing up, there's no way you aren't going to be respected now! As a result, there can be no normal healthy interaction in your home, because everything—and I do mean even the tiniest, unconnected thing—is taken as disrespect and an affront to your authority.

Maybe your father left you and your family when you were young. And you have legitimate, perhaps never even acknowledged deep-seated anger in your heart against him.

Some guys just have a really warped view of masculinity and leadership. They think a whole lot of themselves, and they mistake ego-centered rule for biblical authority. They tell everybody at work what to do and where to get off. Why not at home?

Some guys are surprised at the anger that seems to well up uncontrollably within them. The level of anger they often feel is not equal to the offense. Maybe this is your experience. It's sad to say, but anger is the accepted emotion for men in our culture. So depression and anxiety and disappointment come out as anger. Maybe your father divorced your mom and abandoned you when you were young. Maybe you've had significant disappointments in your career, your marriage, and your financial status. Maybe you struggle big-time with anxiety—the whole world is on your shoulders, and you have never learned to fully trust and rest in God. So it comes out in anger.

We all can explain our anger, but at some point, we have to grow up and become men. We have to get control of our anger. We have to forgive those who have wronged us deeply in the past, so that we can become free of the anger that destroys our sons.

You don't have to be ruled by anger. There is so much hope for you.

With the help of your Father in heaven, you can make a change—a real and genuine change.

> **The fruit of the Spirit is love, joy, peace,** *patience,*
> **kindness, goodness, faithfulness,** *gentleness, self control."*
> **(GALATIANS 5:22–23, italics mine)**

Do you see the words *anger* or *harshness* here? You see *kindness, gentleness, patience, self-control.* So something needs to change.

LEARNING THE CHANGE-UP

How do you change?

Great pitchers have multiple pitches. Curves, sliders, fastballs, fork balls, and split-finger fastballs can all get the job done. But there is no more devastating pitch than a change-up. A change-up looks just like a fastball coming in. The pitcher's motion, the location of his release, and his rhythm look just like the 90 mph fastball. Only it's not coming in at 90; it's coming at 65.

Angry, harsh men have to learn the change-up. And the only way to throw a change-up bibilically is to reverse course.

It's also known as repentance.

And the place to begin is with confession.

Most harsh fathers never get to confession. It's too hard, and they're not tough enough to handle it. So they never do it. William Secker said, "Many blush to confess their faults, who never blush to commit them."

Why is confession so hard? Richard Sibbes nailed it when he remarked that "confession is verbal humiliation." No man wants to humiliate himself. But the fact of the matter is that you have already humiliated yourself if you are constantly harsh. The question is, are you man enough to admit it before God and your family?

FESS UP

Confession. That is a huge word. A powerful word. I think it could also conceivably be one of the most uncomfortable words in the English language. Confession means admission of fault. And we hate more than anything to admit fault. Criminals are encouraged never, ever to confess. Our entire justice system is built upon the premise that any decent criminal is not going to confess. Politicians know that they would be fools to confess any wrongdoing. It could be the end of their careers, and if they protest enough and keep the charade up long enough, people will be far more likely to believe their claims of innocence and move on.

But in the Bible the word *confession* is a healing, transforming word. "Therefore, confess your sins to one another, and pray for one another so that you may be healed" (James 5:16). David experienced the sickness of a stubborn heart, and he also knew the healing power of confession:

> **When I kept silent about my sin, my body wasted away**
> **Through my groaning all day long.**
> **For day and night Your hand was heavy upon me;**
> **My vitality was drained away as with the fever heat of**
> **summer.**
> **I acknowledged my sin to You,**
> **And my iniquity I did not hide....**
> **And You forgave the guilt of my sin.**
> **(PSALM 32:3–5)**

This is what separates the men from the boys. Men can admit when they are wrong.

Confession is a profession of truth. And Satan hates truth. He hates for any man to profess truth. But the truth is that you and I are sinners. We can hardly get up out of bed without sinning. It's woven into our nature, and until we die we will struggle with it. There's nothing weak or unmanly about confessing that truth. In fact, it is the righteous, godly thing to do.

Some of you guys are thinking that you have done irreparable damage already with your sons. But God is gracious. He's in the business of repairing people and relationships. I don't care if you're thirty-five or seventy-five; God wants to help you build a new bridge with your son. And the first brick on that bridge is confession.

What does true confession look like? It goes something like this: "I am sorry. I was wrong. Will you please forgive me for…" (and here's where you specifically name your sin). No excuses. No letting yourself off the hook. If you've just lost it with your son and you say, "I'm sorry that we had an argument," you're letting yourself off the hook. If you say, "I'm sorry I said that, but you (did such and such)," and go on to excuse your behavior by pointing out your son's faults, you're letting yourself off the hook.

Guys, somebody's got to be the man. We have to grow up and be able to say, "I'm sorry. I was wrong. Will you please forgive me for my sin?" and be specific. If you can't say this from deep down in your gut and heart then don't say it at all. No manipulations of people's emotions. No guilt trips on anyone. No sidestepping the conflict or pretending it didn't happen. Only humility and repentance on your part can begin the process of repairing the damage in your family.

You will be amazed at the doors that will open. You cannot fathom the walls and defenses that will come down. The world says, "If you confess, you will disgrace yourself." God says, "If you humble yourself before Me, I will honor and bless you." Listen to Peter, who was constantly sticking his foot in his mouth:

> **Therefore, humble yourselves under the mighty hand of God, that He may exalt you at the proper time, casting all your anxiety on Him, because He cares for you."** (1 PETER 5:6–7)

When a man humbles himself and confesses his faults, an unexpected thing happens. Instead of dishonor comes honor. Instead of disrespect comes respect. Your wife and your children instinctively know that it takes humility to do such a thing. It takes character. And immediately you go up in their eyes. You gain their respect.

So you begin with *confession*.

Then you build a bridge of *communication*.

"LISTENING" COMMUNICATION

Your relationship with your son may be in such bad shape, that he may not grant forgiveness to you. That's okay. He's got to see that what you say is more than just mere words. So now you take the next step. You pursue after him in communication. With one qualification.

It's not *your* communication, but *his*. Your son has to see that your confession is authentic, that he can trust you with his heart, that you love him just the way he is. That you want to know and understand him. And the only way he'll ever believe that is if you *do* understand him.

So here's what you do. You do everything you can to find out what makes your son tick. You remember this don't you? *Let's go through the drill one more time.*

Jesus said that when the one little sheep went missing, the good shepherd left the ninety-nine sheep and went looking for him. A good father pursues after his son.

So here's the drill.

What does your son like to do? Do it with him—whatever it is. We've been over this before but here we go again.

If he likes to camp then take him camping. If he likes to fish, go fishing. If he likes to climb the Alleghenies, climb with him. If he likes to sit in his room and play video games, then do that.

What kind of music does he like to listen to? Then listen to it with him. At this point, you are not listening to critique his music. You are listening to understand *him*. He doesn't value your opinion yet, so hold your tongue, and just listen. He knows you don't like the music. But it would mean a lot to him if you would just listen. If you will just listen, at some point he will open up and tell you why he likes that music. And before you know it, you're connecting.

What is he reading? Get the book and read it.

What are his hobbies? Take time to be interested in what interests him.

Over the course of time, your son will realize *that you are not there to teach him. You're there just because you love him and want to know him.* And at a certain point, you will notice a turn in your relationship. There will be times when you can be vulnerable with him. I remember the day Josh asked me, "Dad, you never worry about anything, do you?" Are you kidding? There was a time in my life when I literally thought I was going to have a heart attack from worry. So I told him a little about that. I noticed a visible relaxation of his muscles. His dad had struggled with worry. Maybe it wasn't so weird to admit that he was worried.

If you will be man enough to put yourself through the humility of confession when you are harsh and overbearing, then you can expect the Lord to do some great things in the future. The day will come when your son—your estranged son—will pick up the phone and call you about a problem he is struggling with. And that's when you'll know that the bridge of communication has finally been completed.

Why? Because you were man enough not to be right about everything. And you admitted it. That's confession. When you are willing to tear yourself down because you deserve it—that's the first step to construction. If you aren't willing to start there, you will continue to crush. And quite frankly, you are without hope.

Construct or crush.

It's your call.

The friendship that can come to an end never really began.

—Pubilius Syrus

GETTING RID OF BAD APPLES

(MENTORING THROUGH FRIENDSHIP)

I NEVER SLEEP ON THE COUCH.

But that night I did.

I'd never slept on that couch before that night and I haven't slept on it since.

But that night I woke up coughing about one o'clock in the morning. I took some stuff, but it wasn't helping. I just kept coughing. About a half hour later, I did something I never do. I got up and went into the living room so that Mary could get some sleep.

Now, interestingly enough, the phone in our bedroom was on the blink. It wasn't working. But because I was on the couch in the living room, I heard the phone ring at two a.m. I wouldn't have heard it if I had been in my bed. But I wasn't in my bed. I was on the couch because little did I know that I needed to be there to get the phone call.

"Hello," I groggily answered.

"Mr. Farrar?"

"Yes."

"This is Officer Smith from the city police department. I'm calling in regard to your son Josh, who is here with me and several other boys at the scene of a party."

"You mean John," I replied.

This was shortly after our son John had come clean about his rebellion.

"No sir, it's Joshua."

"That can't be, Officer. Josh is upstairs in bed. In fact, if you will hold on for a minute, I'll run upstairs and confirm that."

Josh wasn't in his bed. And neither was his friend who was spending the night.

The officer gave me their location and I was there in fifteen minutes.

I will give you the quick version of this story. Josh, who was fourteen at the time, had invited his friend to stay the night. After we had gone to bed, the two of them had decided to do something they had never done. For the first time in his life, Josh decided to sneak out and go to a party. An older teenager who had a car had driven them there. Just as they showed up, some neighbors had called the police and a squad car pulled up. Another kid nearby flicked a small wad of marijuana into the bushes. The officer saw something flying in the air, but didn't see who launched it. After finding the discarded marijuana, he pulled Josh, his friend, and this kid aside. Then he gave me a call.

When I arrived, there was Josh, shoulders slumped and eyes panicked. This officer was great. He picked up on the situation very quickly. He could tell that this was Josh's first departure from the path of righteousness and as a result, the two of us were able to capitalize on the situation for maximum effect.

I later wrote him a letter and thanked him for the way he handled the situation. Between the two of us, we milked this for all it was worth. All three boys denied having had anything to do with it, and so just to help things along a little, I suggested that he should go ahead and just take them all to jail.

That's when the true culprit broke and finally admitted to having the marijuana. The officer took that boy to the station and called his parents. I told the officer that I would take Josh and his friend immediately to the boy's house and inform his parents of what happened. It was three a.m. by the time we walked into the friend's house. His parents came downstairs. His mother, who is a fine woman, was very concerned and involved. As usual, the father was passive.

I told the boys that as of tonight, their friendship was over. They would spend no more time together at all. It was over and done. Final. End of chapter. End of book.

No sooner had we gotten back into the car than Josh broke down. The first words out of his mouth were, "I knew when I left the house that I was going to get caught. I knew it. I absolutely knew it. I knew God wouldn't let me get away with this."

It was John Trapp who said that "conscience is God's spy and man's overseer." As Josh left the house, his conscience was condemning his wrong behavior. And in a matter hours he was found out. That was very gracious of the Lord to providentially work in such a swift manner.

Josh learned a great lesson from all of this. But so did John. When John found out later that morning what had happened with Josh, he was grieved.

John knew that Josh had always been trustworthy up until the previous night. He had been the younger brother of character who had confronted John more than once about the bad choices he saw him making. Now it hit John like a ton of bricks that his bad example was impacting his brother. It was time for him to grow up and make some changes. And this was another foundation stone that the Lord used to bring about a change in John. He suddenly realized the power of example and this influence it can have on someone else.

God brings good out of bad. And he certainly did it in this episode with Josh. There was a genuine brokenness and repentance in Josh. Josh never saw that friend again, other than to speak to him in the hallway at school. Josh realized that he had been pulled in the wrong direction and that he needed to do two things. He needed to choose good friends and he needed to learn to stand alone.

This relationship had developed pretty fast. This friend moved to town just before school started. He had been a nice kid, always respectful toward us. His mom had been thrilled that he had found a Christian friend. But something about him had never sat well with us. He attended church with his mom, but there was an "attitude," a purposeful distance toward us as Josh's parents, a seeming lack of spiritual life. So we kept our eye on him. Soon he became Josh's friend of choice. They had the same interests, the same sense of humor. It was natural for them to do their homework together. They "clicked."

"Where is he with the Lord?" Mary asked Josh one day. "Well, he says he believes, but I don't think he really understands what it means to be a Christian," Josh had answered honestly. "But I'm working on him." The thing was, it looked more like this friend was working on Josh. The more Josh hung around him, the more that "attitude" began to show itself in Josh. We sensed a shift, but we couldn't put our finger on it. It wasn't long before (as Josh later told us) this friend was introducing Josh to some pornographic Web sites . . . just "to see what people talk about." It was at his house when his mother was at home—unknown to her, too, of course. Then came their night out on the town and the end of the friendship.

Sometime later Josh learned that this friend had joined an underground "fight club" that was proving dangerous to his health. He quit going to church altogether and became spiritually hard and cold. Josh realized how alarmingly close he had come to being pulled under. In those few months of friendship, their powerful "connection" had proven to be only a few steps away from his own disconnection from God.

A few brief months.

One bad friend.

That's all it takes to undermine fourteen years of parenting.

Do not be deceived: "Bad company corrupts good morals." (1 CORINTHIANS 15:33)

As a father, you have to be a sentry on the watchtower. We can't let the Enemy inside the camp. If Satan can't get his foot in the door any other way, he can use a friend. This is often the ace that he has hidden up his sleeve.

A good sentry stands guard. He watches. He sees when the enemy is trying to move in. And he knows when to shut the gates. The stakes are high. That's why we've got to know just what we're up against. The teenage years are dangerous. What is remarkable is that teenagers, as we know them today, didn't even exist a hundred years ago. So if you have a teenager, you are dealing with a whole new breed of cat.

THE BIRTH OF THE PEER CLASS

So what has changed in the last one hundred years? Can it really be that big of a deal? A quick look back will help us know what we are up against. Allen Bloom once observed that "we are like ignorant shepherds living on a site where a great civilization once flourished." The issues that fathers deal with today with their teenagers are radically different from one hundred years ago. Yes, there are some issues that would be the same. But a small group of elite educators made a move that hardly anyone noticed. And as result, they set into motion a societal shift that has had huge consequences.

Teenagers have not always existed. At least not as we know them today.

What surprised you most about the *H.M.S. Surprise* when you saw the movie *Master and Commander*? If you didn't see it you should. The *H.M.S. Surprise* is part of a naval fleet of British ships in the early 1800s during the days of the Napoleonic wars. The biggest surprise about the *H.M.S. Surprise* is the age of the young shipmasters on board. We are stunned to see boys who are ten, eleven, twelve years of age and up leading charges in war and learning to navigate warships. Their voices haven't yet changed, yet they are shouting commands.

Patrick O'Brian, writer of the original book, was a premier historian. He was completely accurate in his telling of life as it was in the early 1800s. Young adolescent boys and pre-adolescent boys from well off families were often sent off for apprenticeships aboard ships. And they were expected to learn quickly and work hard. And fight bravely.

Do you have a ten-year-old son? Can you imagine sending him off on a British warship to apprentice under a captain so that he will learn to be a man? Can you imagine your wife letting you send her baby off to a warship knowing full well that it was quite possible that he would be wounded, maimed, or even killed? If I attempted to do that, I would be the one who would be wounded, maimed, and yes, perhaps even killed.

Mothers don't like to send their sons off to war. Especially when they are ten years old. But in the recent past, it was part of how things were done in society.

The mothers hated it. But the boys loved it. They aspired to it. They begged their fathers in many cases to let them go. Others, of course, had no desire to leave home. But that the whole system even existed is a great mystery to us. That was another world.

So how did things change so much from what was common to them to what is common today when it comes to young boys?

THE THREE STAGES

It used to be that there were only three stages of life: childhood, adulthood, and old age. Childhood included *infancy* (when a young boy played at the feet of his mother), *early childhood* (when his little feet and arms were strong enough to help his dad in the field or the shop, and usually ended at the age of six or seven), and *youth* (when a boy moved into training for his life work and finally married).

In his book *The Rise and Fall of the American Teenager*, Thomas Hine describes that world:

> In Massachusetts, for example, military training for boys began at ten. The teenage years were part of a very lengthy, vaguely defined period of youth, which continued, practically speaking, until marriage sometime in one's early to midtwenties. Even people who

held responsible political or military positions tended to be considered youths until they married.

People recognized that this period of youth brought a series of radical changes in size, sexual maturity, and intellectual capability. . . . It may seem ridiculous to us that a ten-year-old and a twenty-year old could be part of the same age group. In the seventeenth century, however, both might work side by side doing the same task, and they would study in the same classroom reading the same books with the same teacher. . . .

A child was wholly dependent on the family, the youth was one who contributed, and an adult was fully capable of forming a new family. There was, officially at least, no such thing as a single person. Each of the New England colonies had laws that forbade living outside the family government . . . . If you did not have a family, the law compelled you to establish living arrangements in a family.[1]

Hine is describing a world in which the path from childhood to adulthood was a series of milestones toward responsibility and maturity. And it started in the preschool years! Even young children were valued as productive, capable contributors to their families and to the world. In other words, nobody was just hanging out. They were working and preparing for life. They were fighting battles and learning trades.

Now here's where it gets interesting. The New England Puritans had a great passion for their families and often wrote very tenderly about their love for their wives and their children. They were concerned that as their sons grew older, their close ties with their sons would tend to make them too soft at a crucial time of maturity. It was common for a father to decide that it was time to send his son away around the age of fourteen.

The Puritans looked for good men who could take their sons to the next step of growth and responsibility. Around the age of fourteen, once a son had shown a leaning toward a particular career "calling," he would leave home to work under a "master." This was an older man who was skilled at his trade or craft.

His master was like a second father, and his master's wife—though not a true mother figure—saw to his physical needs for food and clothing. It was no accident that "mothering" of a son—which was very much valued in his early years—ceased at the age of this threshold into manhood.

Apprenticeship was a mentoring relationship. The master took responsibility not only for training his young charge, but educating him if need be. The law even required masters to make sure their apprentices studied the Christian catechism. If the son attended school, he had to learn well enough to understand the Scriptures. And if a son showed promise for higher education (such as Harvard or Oxford) and the parents could afford it, a tutor would be hired to prepare him.

So, in the time of late childhood, a son was expected to become his own man under the guidance of a mentor. This letter from a Boston father to his son who was about to enter Harvard in 1672 gives you the picture:

> Remember that tho' you have spent your time in the vanity of Childhood; sports and mirth, little minding better things, yet that now, when come to this ripeness of Admission to the College, that now God and man expects you should putt away Childish things: now is the time come wherein you are to be serious, and to learn sobriety, and wisdom in all your ways which concern God and man.[2]

The son was only fourteen years old.

YOUNG AND MARRIED

By the way, it's interesting that in those days sons were marrying at the peak of their sexual maturity. Today our sons are expected to postpone marriage until they are out of college, and oftentimes well beyond. But their sexual drive is not postponed. Let's just lay aside the complete obsession with sex in our culture for a second. Even without that, it shouldn't surprise us that sex is a central issue for our yet unmarried sons in their mid to late twenties.

So what is the point? Until the twentieth century, our sons matured much earlier and were expected to accept responsibility much earlier. And—most importantly—*the primary influence upon their lives* was an older man (first his father and then his mentor) who could lead him into the responsibilities of being a man. That's important!

So what about high school football games, proms, cheerleaders, MTV, gymnastics, select baseball and video games? Quite frankly, all that stuff is what the teenage years are all about today. The whole emphasis is on "fun." But a hundred years ago, the emphasis wasn't on fun. It was on responsibility and how a young man or woman could best learn it. Today the emphasis of the teen culture is on sex. One hundred years ago the focus was on preparing young men and women for marriage.

It wasn't until the twentieth century that a whole new stage of development emerged—the period we now call the teenage period. The first time the term *teenager* was ever used was in 1941, and it really didn't take hold until the 1950s.

The point is this. The modern idea of a teenager is a new development in history. It didn't exist a hundred years ago. But forces began to come into play that gave birth to a new order in families. Essentially, fifty years ago a new approach to maturity and—most importantly—a *new primary influence* upon our sons' maturity took root.

HIGH SCHOOL AND THE COMMITTEE OF TEN

What was the main catalyst? The modern-day high school system.

At the risk of oversimplification, let me bottom-line what happened.

In 1894, a group called the Committee of Ten got together to rethink the way young men and women were educated. It was a prestigious panel of ten men led by Harvard's longtime president Charles William Eliot.[3] They wanted to reshape the thinking behind high school education. They wanted the primary purpose to become preparation for college, and they came up with a four-year curriculum to serve that purpose.[4] They didn't consult with local or rural educators, or businessmen and employers who were hiring the students. And of course they weren't consulting the parents and kids. Instead they consulted with scholars, administrators of colleges and universities, and a few elite secondary school educators. They hoped for a universal experience, with universities setting the standard.

By the 1940s, the high school system conceived by the Committee of Ten was firmly established in our country, and every child was *required* to attend and *expected* to finish. The four-year curriculum they suggested had become the standard. And high schools had turned into large feeder systems where students spent their days with other students exactly their own age, and where their studies were determined by universities and elite educators.

This changed everything. It changed the reason they went to school. It changed the timetable of maturity. (The teenage years became a protracted preparation for college.) It changed the subject matter they studied. It changed who decided what they were to study (putting the responsibility in the hands of an elite few writers of textbooks). We won't even talk about how the approach and curriculum was designed largely on the basis of how girls learn! Most importantly, it changed the primary influence in their lives—which was no longer the family or older close mentors and teachers, but a new family of peers.

Let's stop right there and say that again. It was precisely here that society shifted. This was a big-time earthquake, only no one felt the movement under their feet. This shift in how children were educated took the influence away from parents and the mentors that they chose for their children. With this shift, the influence would now shift from the home to peers, and to a group of "elite" educators, who in time would be proven to have a value system that often undermined what the child was learning in the home.

So by the forties, for the first time in history, kids were spending most of their time inside or outside of school with people their age. They went from being productive people aspiring to the *responsibilities* of adulthood, to dependent consumers aspiring to get out of this transitional world and enjoy the *privileges* of adulthood. The laws actually prevented them from working in the adult world (unless it was in low-paying jobs that adults wouldn't want). Their primary job in life was to study a curriculum which was increasingly irrelevant to their lives and to "find themselves." But how is a son to "find himself" when the primary input that matters to him most is from his peers?

Then we had the great wisdom to force this same approach all the way down to our kindergartners and preschoolers.

It was a total flip-flop. Kids were not expected to grow up so fast.

But they were allowed to actually shape what we value in culture. Now we have parents walking around trying to act and look like teenagers. It's crazy.

Are you kind of getting the picture?

This is the world our sons are growing up in.

We can't change that world. But we can recognize it for what it is. And we can be aware of the options that are available so that we can parent more wisely.

"IN" BUT NOT "OF"

What is a dad to do? Should he remove his son from all contact altogether? I have seen some parents attempt to do that. But if you build an iron curtain, your son will live for the day that he can get over the wall.

On the other hand, you would be foolish to throw all caution to the wind, toss your son to the wolves, and expect him to survive. Just because you grew up a certain way doesn't mean this is how your son should grow up. The world has changed. And believe me, schools and kids have changed. It isn't what it was when you were there. And just because a school hangs out a sign calling itself "Christian" doesn't mean it is a healthy, safe place, or that it is necessarily right for your son. Thankfully, we still live in a free country where parents can decide where they will live and how their children will be educated. It's a great privilege. And you should exercise it well.

So here we are discussing education again. By my count, this is the third time it's come up. Why does it keep coming up? Because it's a mentoring issue! And you've got some options that weren't around just twenty years ago. Home-schooling is an option that more and more parents are taking advantage of. The home-school movement is growing by leaps and bounds, enabling fathers to be more personally involved in their son's education.

Classical Christian schools are popping up everywhere, many of them offering a combination of home-schooling and part-time classical classroom education. These schools are bursting at the seams, as they should be. And they often have strong masculine leadership and teachers that would obviously be a plus for a son's education. The options are continuing to grow and expand as committed Christian parents and educators look for ways to harness technology to the glory of God.

You and your wife need to seriously look at the environment your son is in from dawn until dusk. You've got to find a way to be the primary influence in his early years, and to oversee the primary influences in his life as he steps into manhood. That's what a leader does. You can't afford to make these decisions primarily on the basis of finances or career.

"IN" THE WORLD

On the other hand, your son needs to learn how to function in this world. He's got to learn how to interact socially and winningly, as well as fend for himself as a godly man in an ungodly world. A Christian boy can't live in a Christian cocoon all of his life. Our job as fathers is to equip them to live as Christian men in a non-Christian world. They are to be in the world but not of it.

Jesus put it this way: "Behold, I send you out as sheep in the midst of wolves; so be shrewd as serpents and innocent as doves" (Matthew 10:16).

How do you prepare your son to be thrown to the wolves? You give your son a preseason. Let me explain.

EVERY SON NEEDS A PRESEASON

Bill Parcells is a very successful football coach. Parcells has come up with a fool-proof way to help a young rookie become a professional player. These kids come in from college. They are gifted, and up until now they have been the stars, the big guys on the block. What they don't know is that they are about to have their own blocks knocked off. Some of them have "attitudes." Some of them are lazy. Some of them think far too highly of themselves. That's because they've never run with the wolves.

Parcells' time-worn approach is this: Use the preseason to let them learn a few things. *Throw them in with the wolves*. Give them some playing time with hardcore NFL athletes who will clean their clocks. And then see how they handle it. If they handle it badly, he benches them. They quickly discover that attitude, work ethic, a willingness to learn new things and overcome their weaknesses—these are the deciding factors between those who will make it and those who won't. The next day, they may get another try. But at a certain point, if they refuse to grow and learn, he cuts them. On the other hand, if a player handles himself well, Parcells rewards him by encouraging him at what he has done well. Then he throws him out there the next day with the wolves again.

Your son needs a preseason. He needs the chance to be thrown in with the wolves. By that I mean that *he needs to be given the challenge of mixing it up with the world. He needs to be challenged—while he is still under your roof.* That's why it's called *preseason*. He needs you to gradually (as he matures through adolescence) trust him to make certain decisions—and let him learn from those decisions. He needs certain freedoms. He needs to know that, as he demonstrates wisdom and character, you will trust him to make certain decisions (all the while you are standing watch on the tower). When he's old enough, let him go get a job out there among the wolves. It could be the best experience of his life. Let him play a sport in the "real world" where competition is stiff. Let him go out with good friends—but always know *where* he is going, *who* will be in charge, and *when* he will be home. And then *wait up for him.* (This is some of the best advice I was ever given.) A curfew is meaningless if mom and dad are sound asleep. And for heaven's sake, when the time is right, let him go out on some group dates. Homecoming, proms, and other social high points are great opportunities for your son to prove his godly manhood and have a blast at the same time!

I know that some of you are feeling nervous as you read this. But consider something with me. The tendency for caring, involved Christian parents these days is to *overprotect.* The tendency is to focus so much on our sons *learning* and *doing* what is right that we lose sight of the most important thing of all. What really matters to God is what your son actually believes in his own heart to be true and right. How will he ever know if he is never tested—if he is never in the real world where he is truly in the minority, and his belief system is no longer an intellectual exercise? The decisions your son will eventually make in his life will come from his own *confident* and *tested* convictions. Why not allow the testing and confidence to develop while you still have a close mentoring role in his life?

Junior high and high school are preseason. College and beyond is the real thing, the real game, the "season." If you never allow your son to be in a situation in which his faith is challenged or where his value system is questioned, what's going to happen when he gets out there in the season of real life?

GIVE HIM SOME ROPE

All I am saying to you, guys, is this. Give your son a chance to learn to make his own way. Don't clamp down on him so hard and create such an environment that what comes out will be a "falsely obedient child." These are children who would never disobey at home or screw up at school. They are living out the beliefs of the "majority" around them. Christianity is their comfort zone. My sons, John and Josh, call it "instant gratification obedience." It works for the moment. It works in his home. It works in his protective Christian school. It works in his protective church youth group.

The problem with this kind of obedience is the delayed realizations that will hit him square in the face when he hits the real world. In the real world, he will be in the minority (in every sense of the word, if he holds to biblical Christianity). In the real world, he will be faced by peer pressures like nothing he's known before; he will be tempted in ways he never could have conceived. In other words, when he is in the real world, he is thrown to the wolves. At some point, if your son's faith has never been tested, and especially if he has lived in an overprotective, overcontrolling home, he will hit hard things in life. And the "faith" he may have once apparently embraced (and even championed!) may turn out to have been nothing more than the "means" by which he survived his Christian upbringing.

What I am saying is this. In the midst of his godly training, *give him some rope.* Obviously, be wise about this. Consider his personality and propensities. But let him get out there and make some choices—about where he might go, about how he might spend his time when he is not under your eyes or thumb. Don't control his every living, breathing decision. Encourage opportunities for him to mix it up with the wolves.

Let him experience what it is like to have to stand alone in a world where the majority could care less about his Christian values. And let him make some mistakes!

Haven't you made some mistakes? Did you learn from them? Of course you did. Well, then let him have the same privilege without somebody jumping down his throat. What better time in his life to try some stuff and come up short than under your roof and in close relationship to you, his father and mentor?

And, by the way, when he does make mistakes, don't panic. That's the time he will find out the stuff of which he is made. And you will be there to walk with him through it. If he is repentant—*especially* if he is repentant—reward him for that repentance. Don't clamp down harder on him and crush his spirit further for having repented of a bad choice. Honor him for his repentance, as God honors you for yours.

So give your son a "preseason" chance to mix with the wolves, learn how to make choices for himself, and find out for himself if he really believes what he believes.

Jesus had the great wisdom to pray:

"I do not ask You to take them out of the world, but to keep them from the evil one." (JOHN 17:15)

"In" but not "of." That's the delicate balance.

You and your wife will have to pray and wisely consider how to strike this delicate balance. Our sons have got to learn how to live in an evil world and make good friends. And we've got to help them.

Let me give you a few ideas for accomplishing this tough assignment:

1. Know his friends.

Who is your son hanging out with inside and out of school? Who are his real friends? Do you know them or their families? It takes a lot to stay on top of these things. That's why the more time those kids are in your home, hanging under your roof, the better you will be able to get a handle on that. As much as is possible, make your home the center of activity for your son and his friends.

I once had a ninth grade Christian high school teacher come to me and express concern over a friend of one of my boys. I hardly knew this kid. But my son had begun hanging out with him at school and in after-school sports. And this kid was trouble. I appreciated the heads-up from this teacher that a storm was brewing so that I could head it off at the pass. It didn't take long to find out who he was and to begin to intentionally lead my son away from him. You get my drift.

2. Teach him what a good friend is.

We have to teach our sons about the values and pitfalls of friends. You may not realize this, but your son wants to hear from you. And the earlier you start teaching him, the better. Kindergarten is not too soon.

My sons want friends that they like being around. They've got to be able to laugh and cut loose. I can't blame them. So do I. It's just that having fun can't be the only prerequisite for friendship. Rehoboam had a blast with his friends. They were definitely more hip than his dad's friends. But he forgot his grandfather's words:

> **Blessed is the man who does not walk in the counsel of the wicked, nor stand in the path of sinners, nor sit in the seat of scoffers! (PSALM 1:1)**

And he ignored his father's advice:

He who walks with wise men will be wise,
But the companion of fools will suffer harm.
(PROVERBS 13:20)

So what is the difference between a good and bad friend? Let's toss a few ideas out there:

- *A good friend is like iron sharpening iron (Proverbs 27:17). A bad friend is like rust on iron, corroding whatever it comes in contact with.*
- *A good friend speaks truthfully, but a bad friend "devises violence," and his "lips talk of trouble" (Proverbs 24:1–2).*
- *A good friend is loyal, but a bad friend is fickle (Proverbs 24:21 and 25:19).*
- *A good friend is not driven by instant gratification. But a bad friend says, "Eat, drink, and be merry, for tomorrow we will die!" (Proverbs 23:6, 20–35).*
- *A good friend loves the law of God, but a bad friend is a lawbreaker (Psalm 1:1–2)*

One of the greatest friendships portrayed in Scripture is between David and Jonathan. They were kindred spirits, fiercely loyal and committed to God. Jonathan was a true friend to David. He was more concerned with David's wellbeing than he was with his own. If God had called David to be the next king, then far be it from Jonathan to interfere, even though he was the king's son. What an awesome example of male friendship.

And isn't it interesting that David didn't begin to make serious mistakes in his life until after the death of Jonathan? I have often wondered how different David's life would have been had another friend filled Jonathan's void.

Iron sharpening iron. That's true friendship.

3. Recognize the signs.

There are telltale signs that your son is in a bad friendship. Let me give you some that I have learned through hard experience. If one of these shows up, it's time to prayerfully determine a measured response.

- *He will begin to disconnect from you.* Now if he's smart, he'll do a good job of trying to make you think he is fine. But you will sense the disconnection. A good friend does not cause a son to want to disconnect from his parents.

- *He will become less open about his thoughts and feelings.* A good friend is someone you can confide in. Our kids need to have the freedom to sort things out with their friends. But when your child quits sorting things out with you, he may have switched advisors. You can't force him to open his heart to you, but you can't let him just float away either. This is when you need to do a lot of praying and bridge building. And as you do, just be aware that sometimes secretiveness can be a sign of an unhealthy friendship.

- *He may drop out of life—sports, activities that he has enjoyed, even nose-dive in his schoolwork.* This can be a sign of depression in your son. But it can also be a sign that he has found something more interesting—like being with friends who are up to no good, like drinking or doing drugs. He may tell you he has just lost interest. But take it from those who have worked with teens for years—this is a sure sign of something much deeper.

- *He will develop an "attitude," an air of disdain or disrespect. Or anger.*

We are told today that these attitudes are natural for teens. But if they are, it's because we've allowed them to be.

I heard a great illustration once about rebellion in a child. Rebellion is like a seed. It begins underneath the surface. Rebellion starts in the mind. It's like a seed lying underground, germinating, growing, ruminating. One day the seed gives birth to a decision. "I will act on these feelings," it says. It pops through the surface as a little tiny seedling in the form of "attitude." That's when you first actually see it. And that's when you need to take care of it. If you don't, it will continue to grow and become so entrenched that you can't pull it out by hand. Then you'll need to rent a bush hog to get it out.

But here is my point. If an attitude of rebellion shows up, look around for a friend or friends that are fueling the fire. Germinating and ruminating can be stimulated by a bad friend. And chances are they are right under your nose.

I need to say one more thing here. Just in case you missed the last chapter, the way you root it out is enormously important. This is not the time for a dad to get weird and hard and overcontrolling. This is the time to work your way inside of your son and find out what's really going on. You are stepping up to the plate of his life and letting him know you care deeply about him.

FRIENDS FOR A LIFETIME

A mentor is a friend. And as your son moves into manhood, your discipling role will take a back seat to your friendship. There is nobody your son would rather have for a friend than you. Ask young men anywhere. They'll tell you this is true.

It was C. H. Spurgeon who noted that "friendship is one of the sweetest joys of life. Many might have failed beneath the bitterness of their trial had they not found a friend." Friendship is sweet indeed. And there's nothing sweeter than the friendship of a father and son.

Fathering and mentoring are the work of a man's life.

Richard Monckton Milnes understood this:

> The Christian home is the Master's workshop where the pro-
> cesses of character-molding are silently, lovingly, faithfully and suc-
> cessfully carried on.

On the 8th day of July in the year of 1401, the Dean and Chapel of Seville assembled in the Court of the Elms and solemnly resolved: "Let us build a church so great that those who come after us may think us mad to have attempted it." The church took 150 years to build.[5]

These men took 150 years to build a building. God has not called you to build a building; he has called you to build your son. And you don't have 150 years to get the job done.

You may have eighteen years or you may have eight. Perhaps you have two years, and then he will leave for college. None of us really know how much time we have to build. But what we do know is that we have today.

May God grant you much favor as you put your hand, your heart, and your mind to the task which is worth the effort of a lifetime.

EPILOGUE
A PARTING SHOT

THIS HAS BEEN A BOOK FOR FATHERS AND SONS. SO LET'S GIVE THE girls the last word. In particular, let's give the last word to a little two-year-old girl named Kelsey. Her father, Gary Thomas, tells the story best in his own words. It's a warm story that has a chilling message for every Christian father:

> One day, when our daughter Kelsey was two years old, she started pointing at every family member's chair around the table. I was gone at the time. "Mommy," she began, "Allison, Graham, Kelsey...."
>
> She then pointed to my empty seat and said, "God."
>
> "That's not God, Kelsey," Lisa, my wife said. "That's Papa."
>
> "Jesus," Kelsey replied with a smile.
>
> Three days later, all of us were together in a hotel room when Kelsey did it again. She started pointing to everybody and announc-

ing his or her name. When she got to me, she said, "Jesus."

"I'm not Jesus, Kelsey," I said. "I'm Papa."

"You're Papa God," Kelsey replied.[1]

This little two-year-old girl reminded her father of a great truth. Fathers represent God to their children.

That is why what we do as fathers is so important. How you live your life in private in your own home can affect the entire world.

It is well-known that Adolf Hitler murdered more than six million Jews. His former friend and enemy in Russia was Joseph Stalin. Stalin murdered tens of millions of Russian peasants.

How can two men demonstrate such hatred and rage? What is the explanation for such godless behavior?

It goes back to their fathers.

Hitler was often severely beaten by his father. One beating he took from his father as a young boy was so harsh that it left him in a coma for weeks. The doctors thought he would never recover. But he did.

Stalin's father beat him on a regular basis when he was a young boy growing up. It was common for young Joseph to have blood in his urine. His childhood was characterized by internal bleeding caused by the blows of the most significant man in his life.

These two fathers maimed their sons.

And their sons in turn maimed and murdered millions.

These two fathers would have been shocked beyond belief if someone had told them that their sons would grow up to be monstrous killers. After all, both of these men were "professing" Christians.

But inside their homes they created a living hell for their sons.

God calls fathers not to maim their sons, but to mentor them.

And that is our task and our greatest privilege.

As little Kelsey grows older, she will begin to understand that her daddy is not Jesus.

But down deep in her heart she will always know that her father represents Jesus.

As fathers, we can never lose sight of that truth. It will help us to do our fathering work to the glory of God.

We are to build sons so that they may build their sons.

It is the plan of God. It is your highest earthly calling. There is no work more important.

And you don't have what it takes to pull it off.

Neither do I.

We can't father without the heavenly Father.

But as Francis Schaeffer used to say, "He is there and He is not silent."

Therefore, with his help we can do our fathering work. And we do it to and for his glory.

NOTES

Chapter 1: King Me

1. Alana Nash, "Ties That Bind," *Reader's Digest*, November 2004, 155.

Chapter 2: Building Sons Into Men

1. http://townhall.com/columnists/georgewill/printgw20030921.shtml.
2. Ibid., 2.
3. "Hardwired to Connect: The New Scientific Case for Authoritative Communities, A Report to the Nation from the Commission on Children at Risk," 2003, Institute for American Values, 35.
4. Peter Sprigg and Timothy Dailey, eds., *Getting It Straight: What the Research Shows About Homosexuality* (Washington D.C., Family Research Council, 2004), 113.
5. Josh McDowell, unpublished synopsis of "Hardwired to Connect," 1.
6. Ibid., 1.
7. Dr. James Dobson, *Bringing Up Boys* (Wheaton, IL: Tyndale House, 2001), 33–34.
8. Ibid., 34.
9. Ibid.
10. David McCullough, *Brave Companions* (New York: Touchstone, 1992), 90.

Chapter 3: Rapid Response

1. Alexander Whyte, *Bible Characters from the Old and New Testaments* (Grand Rapids: Kregel, 1990).
2. C. H. Spurgeon, cited by Warren W. Wiersbe, *The Bible Exposition Commentary: Old Testament History* (Colorado Springs: Victor,2003), 361.
3. Ibid., 388.
4. Steve Farrar, *Point Man* (Portland, Ore: Multnomah, 1990), 21.
5. Clifton Fadiman, *The Little, Brown Book of Anecdotes* (Boston: Little, Brown and Company, 1985), 500.
6. Ibid., 76.

Chapter 4: Swift Boot

1. Ulysses S. Grant, *Personal Memoirs* (New York: Random House, 1999), 11.

2. Harold I. Gullan, *First Fathers* (New York: John Wiley, 2004), 110.

3. Robin H. Neillands, *Grant: The Man Who Won the Civil War* (Cold Spring Harbor, N.Y.: Cold Spring, 2004), 17.

4. Jean Edward Smith, *Grant* (New York: Simon and Schuster, 2001), 24.

5. Alexander Whyte, *Bible Characters from the Old and New Testaments* (Grand Rapids: Kregel, 1990), 312–13.

6. Friday, April 9, 2004, *USA Today*, "Before Martha Stewart There Was Chuck Williams," 8D.

7. George Marsden, *Jonathan Edwards: A Life* (New Haven: Yale University Press, 2003), 22.

Chapter 5: Freedom Man

1. Wayne LaPierre, *Guns, Crime and Punishment* (Washington, D.C.: Regnery, 1994), 88.

2. Peggy Noonan, *When Character Was King: A Story of Ronald Reagan* (New York: Penguin, 2001), 314.

Chapter 6: Masculine Sons in a Feminized World

1. Stephen B. Clark, *Man and Woman in Christ* (Ann Arbor, Mich.: Servant, 1980), 636, 638.

2. Ibid., 636.

3. William G. Eberhard, "Under the Influence: Webs and Building Behavior of Plesiometa argyra (Aranea, Tetragnathidae) When Parasitized by Hymenoepimecis argyraphaga," *Journal of Arachnology* 29 (2002): 354–66.

4. Marion J. Levy, as cited by Clark, *Man and Woman in Christ*, 637.

5. George Grant, *Carry a Big Stick* (Nashville: Cumberland, 1996), 96–97.

6. As quoted in Grant, *Carry a Big Stick*, 97.

7. Ibid., 79.

8. Doug Wead, *All the President's Children* (New York: Atria, 2003), 196.

9. Ibid., 197.

10. Ibid., 202.

11. Ibid.

Chapter 7: Why Your Son Exists

1. Stuart Evey, *ESPN: Creating an Empire* (Chicago: Triumph, 2004), 34.

2. Thomas Armstrong, *7 Kinds of Smart* (New York: Plume, 1999).

3. Ibid., p. 149.

4. William Beausay III, *Boys! Shaping Ordinary Boys into Extraordinary Men* (Nashville: Nelson, 1994).

5. I came across this principle of "congruency" in the writings of J. Robert Clinton, particularly in his book *The Making of a Leader* (Colorado Springs: NavPress, 1988).

6. Lee Ellis, *The Pathfinder: A Guide to Career Decision Making* (Gainesville, Ga.: Life Pathways, 1997).

7. Thomas Hine, *The Rise and Fall of the American Teenager* (New York: Perennial, 1999) 66–67.

8. Douglas Wilson, *Restoring the Lost Tools of Education* (Moscow, Idaho: Canon).

Chapter 8: Sons and Sex

1. Thomas Watson, *A Body of Divinity* (Carlisle, Penn., Banner of Truth Trust, 1962), 1.

2. Herbert Lockyer, *All the Men of the Bibles* (Grand Rapids: Zondervan, 1954), 319–20.

3. Dr. James Dobson Jr., *Marriage Under Fire* (Sisters, Oreg., Multnomah, 2004), 8.

4. http://www.guardian.co.uk/print/0,3858,5052158-111675,00.html.

5. Lynne Truss, *Eats, Shoots & Leaves* (New York: Gotham, 2003), back cover.

6. See especially pages 235–47, Steve Farrar, *Point Man* (Sisters, Oreg.: Multnomah, 1990).

Chapter 9: The Kramer of Judah

1. Joseph Epstein, "The Perpetual Adolescent," *The Weekly Standard*, 15 March 2004.

2. Ibid.

3. Ibid.

4. Ibid.

Chapter 10: How To Crush Your Son So He Will Never Recover

1. As quoted in Fritz Rienecker and Cleon Rogers, *Linguistic Key to the Greek New Testament* (Grand Rapids: Zondervan,1976), 582.

Chapter 11: Getting Rid of Bad Apples

1. Thomas Hine, *The Rise and Fall of the American Teenager* (New York, NY: Perennial, 1999).

2. Ibid.

3. http://www.blancmange.net/tmh/books/commoften/mainrpt.html.

4. http://www.nd.edu/~rbarger/www7/neacom10.html.

5. John W. Gardner, *The Task of Motivating* (Washington, D.C.: Independent Sector, 1988), 7.

Chapter 12: Epilogue

1. Gary L. Thomas, *Sacred Parenting* (Grand Rapids: Zondervan, 2004), 11.

STEVE FARRAR
IN PERSON — IN YOUR CITY

Steve Farrar's Men's Leadership Conference

Thousands of men have discovered that, as in the pages of his books, Steve Farrar also shoots straight in person. His Men's Leadership Conferences are held all across America to equip men to be better husbands, better fathers, better grandfathers, and more effective spiritual leaders.

CONFERENCE TOPICS:

- *How to Be a Godly Leader*
- *How to Discern the Culture Today*
- *How to Spiritually Lead Your Family*
- *How to Be a Godly Husband*
- *How to Raise Masculine Sons and Feminine Daughters*
- *How to Be a Godly Father and Grandfather*
- *How to Finish Strong in the Christian Life*

Steve Farrar is right on target, he understands our times, he talks straight, he doesn't mess around and best of all, he walks the talk!
— CHUCK SWINDOLL, *Insight for Living*

For more information about attending or hosting a conference, call
1-800-MEN-LEAD
or visit us at WWW.STEVEFARRAR.COM

S ince 1894, Moody Publishers has been dedicated to equip and motivate people to advance the cause of Christ by publishing evangelical Christian literature and other media for all ages, around the world. Because we are a ministry of the Moody Bible Institute of Chicago, a portion of the proceeds from the sale of this book go to train the next generation of Christian leaders.

If we may serve you in any way in your spiritual journey toward understanding Christ and the Christian life, please contact us at *www.moodypublishers.com.*

"All Scripture is God-breathed and is useful for teaching, rebuking, correcting and training in righteousness, so that the man of God may be thoroughly equipped for every good work."
— 2 Timot h y 3:16, 17

MOODY
PUBLISHERS
THE NAME YOU CAN TRUST.

KING ME TEAM

ACQUIRING EDITOR
Mark Tobey

BACK COVER COPY
Laura Pokrzywa

COPY EDITOR
Jim Vincent

COVER DESIGN
The DesignWorks Group, Charles Brock
www.designworksgroup.com

COVER PHOTO
Steve Gardner/pixelworksstudio.net

INTERIOR DESIGN
Smartt Guys

PRINTING AND BINDING
Lake Book Manufacturing, Inc.

The typeface for the text of this book is
Dante